A CENTENNIAL CELEBRATION

A CENTENNIAL CELEBRATION

Recipes from Solo

Solo/Baker Brand
A division of Sokol and Company

On the Cover: Marzipan fruit (pages 146-47), Marzipan Truffles (pages 144-45), Caramel Crunch Apples (page 138), Glazed Fruit "Pizza" (page 126), Spitzer's Torte (page 121), Poppy Seed Quick Bread (page 14), European Kolacky (page 67)

Project Directors: Jack Novak, Bill Dahle
Home Economist: Jean Jervis
Recipe Consultant: Mary Ann Sadilek
Recipe Development: Sokol and Company and International
   Cookbook Services
Senior Editor: Barbara Bloch
Food Stylist: Rita Barrett
Photography: Bob Buchanan
Art and Design: Tom Brecklin, Christine Coleman

Produced and published by The Benjamin Company, Inc.
One Westchester Plaza
Elmsford, NY 10523

The following trademarks appearing in this centennial cookbook are owned by and identified products of Sokol and Company: Solo, Baker Brand.

Library of Congress Catalog Card Number: 88-70392

ISBN: 0-87502-229-4

Printed and bound in the United States of America
First printing: August 1988

CONTENTS

Hello. Welcome to the kitchens of Sokol and Company. And thank you for inviting us into *your* kitchen, through the pages of this centennial collection of famous recipes from the Sokol family of Solo and Baker Brand products.

Of course, our products are no strangers to the kitchens of America's homemakers. It's been nearly 100 years since John A. Sokol established the traditions that make our company a leader in the production of taste-tempting, high-quality foods. Through the years, four generations of American cooks have come to rely on Solo products for adding that special touch of perfection to their baking and cooking. Today you too expect the best from every container of Solo and Baker cake, pastry, and dessert fillings, nut and fish pastes, fruit glazes, dessert toppings, and dressings. And we're able to bring you the best because over the past century, we've never wavered in our commitment to one guiding principle: to put the most creative people, the latest technology, and the finest ingredients to work in constantly improving our food products and developing new products to meet America's changing needs and tastes.

We're very proud to bring you our centennial selection of favorite recipes – the largest collection ever of recipes featuring Solo and Baker products. You'll find yeast breads, quick breads, muffins, cookies, pies, pastries, cakes, and other dazzling desserts, as well as a tantalizing assortment of appetizers, main dishes, and salads. Many recipes are the time-tested treasures that used to fill Grandma's kitchen with tantalizing aromas. Others are brand-new creations developed with ease of preparation and extra-special flavor. Some recipes are especially simple to make or take just a few minutes to prepare – we've pointed those out with a *Quick* or *Easy* tag. All recipes have been carefully tested and refined by specially trained home economists in our Sokol test kitchen. Each promises you the sure, sweet taste of success because it's based on only the best – the consistently high-quality products from Sokol and Company.

We hope you'll enjoy preparing and serving Traditional Almond Kringle, Solo Poppy Cake, European Kolacky, and many other traditional favorites filled with old-fashioned goodness and flavor but presented with a new twist – modern convenience and quick, easy preparation. Or try your hand at contemporary creations like Apricot Brie in Puff Pastry, Glazed Fruit "Pizza," and Raspberry Yogurt Dessert Soup, or the taste-tempting recipes that feature our Solo Fruit Salad Dressing. To help you start thinking of delicious new ways to use that Solo or Baker can or jar on your shelf, we've included a unique feature at the back of this book – a separate product index. Just look for the specific Solo or Baker product name and you'll find a listing of every recipe in the book that contains that product. And remember, whether you reach for the familiar Solo can or open a jar of fine baking or dessert products from Baker – a distinctive member of the Sokol family since 1983 – you're assured of the same delectable taste and dependable quality. That's because we've never wavered in our commitment to continue improving our standards and developing new products to meet your changing needs. We *never* compromise on quality. And neither should you!

To your family from the Sokol family, our thanks. We look forward, with great pride and pleasure, to another century of serving only the best to you and yours.

Sara Solo

CHAPTER 1

Quick Breads
and
Muffins

*Almond Loaf, Apple Crumb
Cake (page 10)*

ALMOND LOAF

1 can Solo Almond Paste
¾ cup butter or margarine, softened
¾ cup sugar
3 eggs
2 teaspoons baking powder
2 cups all-purpose flour

¼ cup milk
½ cup chopped nuts, raisins, or
candied cherries
⅓ cup Solo Toasted Almond Crunch
Topping

Preheat oven to 350°F. Grease 9 x 5-inch loaf pan and set aside.

Break almond paste into small pieces and place in medium-size bowl or container of food processor. Add butter and beat with electric mixer or process until mixture is creamy and smooth. Add sugar and eggs and beat or process until thoroughly blended. (If using food processor, transfer mixture to medium-size bowl.)

Stir baking powder into flour. Add to almond mixture alternately with milk, beating until blended. Fold in chopped nuts. Pour into prepared pan and sprinkle toasted almond crunch topping over batter.

Bake 60 to 70 minutes or until cake tester inserted in center comes out clean. Cool in pan on wire rack 10 minutes. Remove from pan and cool completely on rack.

1 loaf   *(see photo pages 8-9)*

APPLE CRUMB CAKE

Crumb Topping:

½ cup all-purpose flour
¼ cup firmly packed brown sugar
¼ cup granulated sugar

½ teaspoon cinnamon
¼ cup butter or margarine

Cake:

⅓ cup butter or margarine, softened
½ cup granulated sugar
2 eggs
1½ cups all-purpose flour
1½ teaspoons baking powder
1 teaspoon grated lemon peel

½ teaspoon cinnamon
½ cup milk
1 can Solo or 1 jar Baker Apple
Filling
Confectioners sugar

Preheat oven to 350°F. Grease 9-inch square baking pan and set aside.

To make crumb topping, stir flour, sugars, and cinnamon in small bowl. Cut in butter until mixture resembles coarse crumbs. Set crumb topping aside.

To make cake, beat butter and granulated sugar in medium-size bowl with electric mixer until light and fluffy. Add eggs and beat until blended. Stir flour, baking powder, lemon peel, and cinnamon until mixed. Add to butter mixture alternately with milk, beating until blended.

Spread batter evenly in prepared pan. Spread apple filling over batter and sprinkle reserved crumb topping over apple filling.

Bake 30 to 35 minutes or until toothpick inserted in center comes out clean. Cool completely in pan on wire rack. Dust with confectioners sugar and cut into nine 3-inch squares. May be served warm, omitting confectioners sugar.

9 servings   *(see photo pages 8-9)*

CARROT NUT BREAD

½ cup raisins
3 tablespoons boiling water
2 eggs
⅓ cup vegetable oil
1 cup sugar
1 can Solo or 1 jar Baker Nut Filling
1¾ cups all-purpose flour

1 teaspoon baking soda
1 teaspoon cinnamon
½ teaspoon baking powder
½ teaspoon nutmeg
½ teaspoon allspice
1 cup grated or shredded carrots

Preheat oven to 350°F. Grease 9 x 5-inch loaf pan and set aside.

Place raisins in small bowl and stir in boiling water. Set aside.

Beat eggs, oil, and sugar in large bowl with electric mixer until blended. Beat in nut filling. Stir flour, baking soda, cinnamon, baking powder, nutmeg, and allspice until mixed. Add to egg mixture and stir until dry ingredients are moistened. Fold in carrots and raisins and pour into prepared pan.

Bake 55 to 60 minutes or until cake tester inserted in center comes out clean. Cool in pan on wire rack 10 minutes. Remove from pan and cool completely on rack.

1 loaf

DATE BANANA BREAD

⅓ cup butter or margarine, melted
½ cup sugar
2 eggs
1 can Solo or 1 jar Baker Date
    Filling
1⅓ cups mashed bananas (about
    3 medium-size bananas)

2 cups all-purpose flour
2 teaspoons baking powder
½ teaspoon baking soda
½ teaspoon salt
½ teaspoon cinnamon
¼ teaspoon nutmeg

Preheat oven to 350°F. Grease 9 x 5-inch loaf pan and set aside.

Beat butter and sugar in medium-size bowl with electric mixer until blended. Add eggs, date filling, and bananas, and beat until combined. Stir flour, baking powder, baking soda, salt, cinnamon, and nutmeg until mixed. Add to date mixture and stir until dry ingredients are moistened. Pour into prepared pan.

Bake 60 to 70 minutes or until cake tester inserted in center comes out clean. Cool in pan on wire rack 10 minutes. Remove from pan and cool completely on rack.

1 loaf

BERRY CHIP LOAF

⅓ cup butter or margarine, softened
½ cup sugar
2 eggs
1 teaspoon vanilla
2 cups all-purpose flour
2½ teaspoons baking powder
½ teaspoon salt
¼ teaspoon baking soda

½ cup milk
1 can Solo or 1 jar Baker Raspberry
  or Strawberry Filling
4 squares (4 ounces) semisweet
  chocolate, finely chopped, or
  ⅔ cup mini semisweet chocolate
  morsels

Preheat oven to 325°F. Grease 9 x 5-inch loaf pan and set aside.

Beat butter and sugar in medium-size bowl with electric mixer until light and fluffy. Add eggs and vanilla and beat until blended. Stir flour, baking powder, salt, and baking soda until mixed. Add to butter mixture alternately with milk, beating until blended. Fold in raspberry filling and chocolate and spread batter in prepared pan.

Bake 1 hour 20 minutes to 1 hour 25 minutes or until cake tester inserted in center comes out clean. Cool in pan on wire rack 10 minutes. Remove from pan and cool completely on rack.

1 loaf

APPLE RAISIN LOAF

2 eggs
3 tablespoons vegetable oil
⅔ cup sugar
1 can Solo or 1 jar Baker Apple
  Filling
¾ cup lemon-flavored or plain yogurt
2 cups all-purpose flour

2 teaspoons baking powder
1 teaspoon baking soda
1 teaspoon cinnamon
1 teaspoon nutmeg
½ teaspoon salt
¼ teaspoon ground cloves
½ cup raisins

Preheat oven to 350°F. Grease 9 x 5-inch loaf pan and set aside.

Beat eggs, oil, and sugar in medium-size bowl with electric mixer until blended. Stir in apple filling and yogurt. Stir flour, baking powder, baking soda, cinnamon, nutmeg, salt, and cloves until mixed. Add to apple mixture and stir until blended. Fold in raisins and pour into prepared pan.

Bake 65 to 70 minutes or until cake tester inserted in center comes out clean. Cool in pan on wire rack 10 minutes. Remove from pan and cool completely on rack.

1 loaf

Quick # QUICK PRUNE BRAID

2 cans (8 ounces each) refrigerated
    crescent dinner rolls
1 can Solo or 1 jar Baker Prune
    Filling

⅓ cup finely chopped walnuts or
    pecans
1 teaspoon grated lemon or orange
    peel
½ teaspoon cinnamon

Glaze:
1 cup confectioners sugar   1 to 2 tablespoons milk

Preheat oven to 375°F.

Unroll dough and separate each package of dough into 4 rectangles. (Do not separate into triangles.) Place the 8 rectangles, wide edges slightly overlapping, on large ungreased baking sheet to make 13 x 15-inch rectangle. Press edges of dough firmly together to seal.

Combine prune filling, walnuts, lemon peel, and cinnamon in small bowl. Spread prune mixture lengthwise down center of dough in 3-inch-wide strip. Make cuts in from edges almost to filling about 2 inches apart down both sides of dough. Fold strips of dough halfway over filling, 1 at a time, alternating right side and left side. Slant strips slightly downward so ends touch. Pinch and tuck ends under at top and bottom to seal.

Bake 15 to 20 minutes or until golden brown. Remove from baking sheet and cool completely on wire rack.

To make glaze, combine confectioners sugar and milk in small bowl and stir until smooth. Spoon or drizzle glaze over braid. Let stand until glaze is set.

1 braid

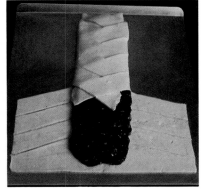

1: *Cut dough into diagonal strips, about 2 inches apart, down each side.*

2: *Fold alternating strips of dough over filling.*

Easy POPPY SEED QUICK BREAD

1 can Solo or 1 jar Baker Poppy Filling	1½ cups sugar
4 eggs	1 teaspoon vanilla
1 cup vegetable oil	5 teaspoons baking powder
1 can (12 ounces) evaporated milk	½ teaspoon salt
	4 cups all-purpose flour

Preheat oven to 350°F. Grease two 9 x 5-inch loaf pans and set aside.

Beat poppy filling, eggs, oil, evaporated milk, sugar, and vanilla in large bowl with electric mixer at low speed until well blended. Stir baking powder and salt into flour. Add to poppy mixture gradually, and beat at medium speed until blended. Beat 2 minutes. Pour into prepared pans.

Bake 55 to 65 minutes or until cake tester inserted in center comes out clean. Cool in pans on wire racks 10 minutes. Remove from pans and cool completely on racks.

2 loaves

Quick QUICK SOLO COFFEE CAKE

2 cups buttermilk baking mix	¼ cup confectioners sugar
½ cup granulated sugar	½ teaspoon cinnamon
1 egg	¼ teaspoon allspice
⅔ cup milk	1½ tablespoons butter or margarine
1 can Solo or 1 jar Baker Filling (any flavor)	

Preheat oven to 400°F. Grease 9-inch square baking pan and set aside.

Stir buttermilk baking mix and granulated sugar in medium-size bowl until blended. Beat egg and milk until blended. Add to dry ingredients and stir just until moistened. Spread batter in prepared pan. Spread filling over batter and swirl through batter with flat-bladed knife for marble effect. Combine confectioners sugar, cinnamon, and allspice in small bowl. Sprinkle over top of cake and dot with butter.

Bake 25 to 30 minutes or until cake tester inserted in center comes out clean. Cool in pan on wire rack 10 minutes. Cut into nine 3-inch squares and serve warm.

9 servings

LEMON NUT BREAD

2¼ cups all-purpose flour
⅔ cup sugar
1 tablespoon baking powder
1 tablespoon grated lemon peel
½ teaspoon baking soda
½ teaspoon salt
2 eggs

⅓ cup vegetable oil
⅓ cup lemon juice
⅓ cup orange juice
1 can Solo or 1 jar Baker Nut Filling or 1 can Solo Pecan Filling

Preheat oven to 350°F. Grease 9 x 5-inch loaf pan and set aside.

Stir flour, sugar, baking powder, lemon peel, baking soda, and salt in medium-size bowl. Beat eggs, oil, lemon juice, and orange juice with electric mixer until blended. Add to dry ingredients and stir until blended. Stir in nut filling and pour into prepared pan.

Bake 60 to 65 minutes or until cake tester inserted in center comes out clean. Cool in pan on wire rack 10 minutes. Remove from pan and cool completely on rack.

1 loaf

Quick POPPY HORNS

2 cans (8 ounces each) refrigerated crescent dinner rolls

1 can Solo or 1 jar Baker Poppy Filling

Glaze:
½ cup confectioners sugar
1 to 1½ tablespoons milk

¼ teaspoon grated lemon peel

Preheat oven to 375°F. Grease large baking sheet and set aside.

Separate dough along perforations into 16 triangles. Spread poppy filling over triangles. Roll up, starting at wide end. Place, pointed end down, on prepared baking sheet.

Bake 12 to 14 minutes or until golden brown. Remove from baking sheet and cool on wire rack 5 minutes.

To make glaze, combine confectioners sugar, milk, and lemon peel in small bowl, and stir until smooth. Drizzle glaze over top of horns while still warm. Let stand until glaze is set.

16 horns

QUICK

QUICK MUFFINS

	POPPY	DATE	APPLE	PECAN	PINEAPPLE
Buttermilk baking mix	2 cups	2 cups	2 cups	2 cups	2 cups
Granulated sugar	½ cup	½ cup	½ cup	½ cup	½ cup
Brown sugar	–	⅓ cup	–	⅓ cup	3 tablespoons*
Chopped nuts	½ cup	½ cup	–	⅓ cup	–
Lemon peel	½ teaspoon	–	–	–	1 teaspoon
Cinnamon	–	–	1 teaspoon	–	–
Nutmeg	–	–	½ teaspoon	–	–
Eggs	2	2	2	2	2
Vegetable or corn oil	5 tablespoons	5 tablespoons	5 tablespoons	5 tablespoons	5 tablespoons
Buttermilk	⅔ cup	⅔ cup	⅔ cup	⅔ cup	⅔ cup
Solo or Baker Filling	1 container	1 container	1 container	1 container	1 container

Preheat oven to 400°F. Line one 12-cup and one 6-cup muffin pan with cupcake liners or spray pans with non-stick cooking spray. Set aside.

Stir baking mix, sugar(s), (nuts and lemon peel or spices, if using) until blended. Beat eggs, oil, and buttermilk with electric mixer until blended. Add to dry ingredients and stir just until moistened. (Batter will be lumpy.) Stir in filling. Spoon batter into prepared muffin cups, filling cups about two-thirds full.

Bake 15 to 18 minutes or until toothpick inserted in center of muffin comes out clean. Cool in pans on wire racks 1 minute. Remove from pans and serve warm or cool completely on racks.

Note: Brown sugar in pineapple muffins is sprinkled over muffins just before baking. Muffins may be served with Fruit Butter (page 21).

Pecan Muffins, Poppy Muffins, Apple Muffins (opposite), Apricot Crumb Muffins (page 18)

APRICOT CRUMB MUFFINS

Crumb Topping:

¼ cup all-purpose flour
3 tablespoons brown sugar

2 tablespoons butter or margarine,
softened

Muffins:

2 cups all-purpose flour
⅔ cup granulated sugar
1 tablespoon baking powder
1 teaspoon cinnamon
½ teaspoon salt
1 egg

3 tablespoons vegetable oil
¾ cup orange juice
1 can Solo or 1 jar Baker Apricot
Filling
½ cup chopped pecans

Preheat oven to 400°F. Line 12-cup muffin pan with paper cupcake liners and set aside.

To make crumb topping, stir flour and brown sugar in small bowl. Cut in butter until mixture resembles coarse crumbs and set aside.

To make muffins, stir flour, granulated sugar, baking powder, cinnamon, and salt in medium-size bowl until blended. Beat egg, oil, and orange juice in separate bowl until blended. Make well in center of dry ingredients and pour in egg mixture. Stir just until dry ingredients are moistened. Stir in apricot filling and pecans. Spoon batter into prepared muffin cups, filling cups about three-fourths full. Sprinkle reserved crumb topping over muffins.

Bake 20 to 22 minutes or until toothpick inserted in center of muffin comes out clean. Cool in pan on wire rack 5 minutes. Remove from pan and serve warm or cool completely on rack.

12 muffins   *(see photo page 16)*

HI-FIBER DATE MUFFINS

½ cup all-purpose flour
½ cup whole-wheat flour
½ cup wheat germ or unprocessed
bran
½ cup all-bran cereal
1 tablespoon baking powder
¼ teaspoon salt

¼ cup vegetable oil
½ cup firmly packed brown sugar
1 egg
¼ cup milk
1 can Solo or 1 jar Baker Date
Filling

Preheat oven to 375°F. Grease 12-cup muffin pan and set aside.

Stir flours, wheat germ, all-bran cereal, baking powder, and salt in medium-size bowl until blended, and set aside. Beat oil, brown sugar, egg, milk, and date filling in medium-size bowl with electric mixer until well blended. Make well in center of dry ingredients and add date mixture. Stir with wooden spoon until thoroughly combined. Spoon into prepared muffin cups, filling cups about two-thirds full.

Bake 18 to 22 minutes or until toothpick inserted in muffin comes out clean. Cool in pan on wire rack 5 minutes. Remove from pan and serve warm or cool completely on rack.

12 muffins

CHERRY NUT MUFFINS

2 cups all-purpose flour
½ cup sugar
1 tablespoon baking powder
1 teaspoon grated orange peel
½ teaspoon salt

⅓ cup vegetable oil
½ cup milk
2 eggs
1 can Solo or 1 jar Baker Cherry Filling
½ cup chopped walnuts or pecans

Preheat oven to 375°F. Grease 12-cup muffin pan and set aside.

Stir flour, sugar, baking powder, orange peel, and salt in medium-size bowl until blended. Set aside.

Place oil, milk, and eggs in small bowl and beat with wire whisk until blended. Add to flour mixture and stir just until dry ingredients are moistened. Stir in cherry filling and nuts. Spoon batter into prepared muffin cups, filling cups three-fourths full.

Bake 20 to 25 minutes or until toothpick inserted in center of muffin comes out clean. Cool in pan on wire rack 2 minutes. Remove from pan and cool on rack 5 to 10 minutes. Serve muffins warm.

12 muffins

BLUEBERRY MUFFINS

2 cups all-purpose flour
½ cup firmly packed brown sugar
2½ teaspoons baking powder
½ teaspoon salt
½ teaspoon cinnamon

½ teaspoon nutmeg
½ cup milk
⅓ cup vegetable oil
2 eggs
1 can Solo or 1 jar Baker Blueberry Filling

Preheat oven to 375°F. Grease 12-cup muffin pan and set aside.

Stir flour, brown sugar, baking powder, salt, cinnamon, and nutmeg in medium-size bowl until blended and set aside.

Place milk, oil, and eggs in small bowl and beat with wire whisk until well blended. Add to flour spice mixture and stir just until dry ingredients are moistened. Stir in blueberry filling. Spoon batter into prepared muffin cups, filling cups three-fourths full.

Bake 20 to 25 minutes or until toothpick inserted in center of muffin comes out clean. Cool in pan on wire rack 2 minutes. Remove from pan and cool on rack 5 to 10 minutes. Serve muffins warm.

12 muffins

Easy   # FRENCH TOAST
WITH BLUEBERRY CREAM

Blueberry Cream:

1 cup heavy cream
1 to 2 tablespoons confectioners
  sugar

1 teaspoon grated lemon peel
1 can Solo or 1 jar Baker Blueberry,
  Raspberry, or Strawberry Filling

French Toast:

6 eggs
½ cup milk
¼ teaspoon nutmeg

⅛ teaspoon cinnamon
8 slices white bread
Butter or margarine for frying

Beat cream in large bowl with electric mixer until soft peaks form. Add confectioners sugar and lemon peel and beat until firm. Fold whipped cream into blueberry filling and refrigerate while preparing French Toast.

To make French Toast, beat eggs, milk, nutmeg, and cinnamon in shallow dish until foamy. Add bread, 1 or 2 slices at a time, and turn to coat both sides.

Melt 1 or 2 tablespoons butter in large skillet over medium heat. Add 2 soaked slices of bread and fry 3 to 4 minutes on each side or until golden brown. Repeat with remaining bread, adding more butter to skillet as necessary.

Serve warm, topped with Blueberry Cream.

4 servings

PRUNE WALNUT BREAD

2 cups all-purpose flour
1 tablespoon baking powder
1 teaspoon cinnamon
½ teaspoon nutmeg
½ teaspoon salt
1 cup firmly packed brown sugar

1 egg
1 can Solo or 1 jar Baker Prune or
  Date Filling
¾ cup milk
⅓ cup vegetable oil
½ cup coarsely chopped walnuts

Preheat oven to 350°F. Grease 9 x 5-inch loaf pan and set aside.

Stir flour, baking powder, cinnamon, nutmeg, and salt in medium-size bowl and set aside.

Beat brown sugar and egg in large bowl with electric mixer until blended. Add prune filling, milk, and oil, and beat until blended. Add reserved dry ingredients and stir just until moistened. Stir in walnuts. Pour into prepared pan.

Bake 50 to 60 minutes or until cake tester inserted in center comes out clean. Cool in pan on wire rack 10 minutes. Remove from pan and cool completely on rack.

1 loaf

WAFFLES WITH FRUIT BUTTER

1¾ cups all-purpose flour
2 to 3 tablespoons sugar
1 tablespoon baking powder
1 teaspoon salt
2 eggs, separated

⅓ cup vegetable oil, melted butter, or margarine
1½ cups milk or half and half
Fruit Butter (recipe follows)

Preheat waffle iron according to manufacturer's instructions.

Stir flour, sugar, baking powder, and salt in medium-size bowl. Beat egg yolks, oil, and milk. Add to dry ingredients and stir well. Beat egg whites in separate bowl with electric mixer until soft peaks form. Fold into batter. Pour batter into pitcher or large measuring cup.

Pour batter in center of waffle iron, filling iron about half full. Cook according to manufacturer's instructions. Repeat with remaining batter. Serve warm with Fruit Butter.

8 waffles

Fruit Butter:

½ cup unsalted butter, softened

1 can Solo or 1 jar Baker Strawberry, Raspberry, Cherry, Apricot, Pineapple, or Prune Filling

Beat butter in medium-size bowl with electric mixer until creamy and fluffy. Add strawberry filling, one-third at a time, beating constantly until thoroughly blended. Spoon into serving dish, cover with plastic wrap, and refrigerate or freeze until ready to use.

About 1½ cups

Note: Do not substitute salted butter or margarine for unsalted butter in Fruit Butter recipe. Fruit Butter may be served with waffles, pancakes, muffins, or on toast.

Baking with Yeast

Poppy Roll (page 24),
Nut Braid (page 25)

POPPY ROLL

About 3¼ cups all-purpose flour	½ cup butter or margarine
2 tablespoons sugar	2 eggs
½ teaspoon salt	1 can Solo or 1 jar Baker Poppy or
1 package active dry yeast	Nut Filling
½ cup dairy sour cream	Confectioners sugar
¼ cup water	

Combine 1 cup flour, sugar, salt, and yeast in large bowl and stir until blended. Place sour cream, water, and butter in small saucepan. Cook over low heat until very warm (120°F-130°F). Add to dry ingredients gradually and beat with electric mixer at low speed until blended. Increase speed to medium and beat 2 minutes. Beat in eggs and ½ cup flour. Beat 2 minutes. Stir in enough remaining flour to make soft dough. Turn out onto lightly floured surface and knead until smooth and elastic, about 5 to 8 minutes. Cover with towel and let rest 10 minutes.

Grease large baking sheet.

Punch dough down and divide in half. Roll out 1 piece of dough on lightly floured surface to 12 x 14-inch rectangle. Spread half of poppy filling over dough to within ½ inch of edges all the way around. Roll up dough, jelly-roll style, starting from long side. Pinch seam to seal. Place filled roll, seam side down, on prepared baking sheet. Repeat with remaining dough and filling. Cover with towel and set aside in warm, draft-free place to rise until almost doubled in bulk, about 45 minutes.

Preheat oven to 350°F.

Bake 30 to 35 minutes or until lightly browned. Remove from baking sheet and cool completely on wire rack. Dust with confectioners sugar before serving.

2 rolls (10 to 12 servings each)   *(see photo page 22)*

BASIC SWEET DOUGH FOR COFFEE CAKES

About 3½ cups all-purpose flour	¼ cup butter or margarine
¼ cup sugar	1 cup milk, light cream, or half and
1 package active dry yeast	half
1 teaspoon salt	3 egg yolks

Combine 1½ cups flour, sugar, yeast, and salt in large bowl, and stir until blended. Place butter and milk in small saucepan. Cook over low heat until very warm (120°F-130°F). Add to dry ingredients gradually, beating with electric mixer at low speed until blended. Increase speed to medium and beat 2 minutes. Add egg yolks and 1 cup flour and beat 2 minutes. Stir in enough remaining flour to make stiff dough. Turn out onto lightly floured surface and knead until smooth and elastic, 5 to 8 minutes.

Place dough in greased bowl and turn to coat entire surface of dough. Cover with towel and set aside in warm, draft-free place to rise until doubled in bulk, about 1 hour.

Punch dough down and use in recipes that follow or in other coffee cake recipes.

1 large coffee cake (10 to 12 servings)

REFRIGERATOR DOUGH

About 5½ cups all-purpose flour   **1½ cups milk**
½ cup sugar   **¼ cup butter or margarine**
2 packages active dry yeast   **2 eggs**
1 teaspoon salt

Combine 2 cups flour, sugar, yeast, and salt in large bowl, and stir until blended. Place milk and butter in small saucepan. Cook over low heat until very warm (120°F-130°F). Add to dry ingredients gradually, beating with electric mixer at low speed until blended. Increase speed to medium and beat 2 minutes. Add eggs and 1½ cups flour and beat on high 2 minutes. Stir in enough remaining flour to make stiff dough. Turn out onto lightly floured surface and knead until smooth and elastic, 8 to 10 minutes.

Cover dough with plastic wrap and cover wrap with towel. Let rest 30 minutes.

Use dough in recipes that follow, or grease baking sheet, cut dough in half, shape each half, and fill with desired filling. Place on prepared baking sheet and let rise in refrigerator 2 to 24 hours. Bake as directed in recipe.

2 coffee cakes (8 to 10 servings each)

NUT BRAID

1 recipe Basic Sweet Dough for
  Coffee Cakes (page 24)
1 can Solo or 1 jar Baker Almond or
  Nut Filling or 1 can Solo Pecan
  Filling

1 egg yolk beaten with 1 tablespoon
  milk for brushing

Glaze:
1 cup confectioners sugar   **1 to 2 tablespoons milk or half and**
    half

Preheat oven to 375°F. Grease baking sheet and set aside.

Punch dough down and divide into 3 equal-size pieces. Roll out 1 piece of dough on lightly floured surface to 10 x 16-inch rectangle. Spread one-third of almond filling over dough to within ½ inch of edges all the way around. Roll up dough, jelly-roll style, starting from long side. Pinch seam to seal. Repeat with remaining dough and almond filling.

Place filled rolls on prepared baking sheet, pinch top ends of rolls together, and braid. Pinch and tuck bottom ends under and brush braid with beaten egg yolk mixture.

Bake 30 to 35 minutes or until deep golden brown. Remove from baking sheet and cool completely on wire rack.

To make glaze, combine confectioners sugar and milk in small bowl and stir until smooth. Drizzle over braid in zig-zag pattern. Let stand until glaze is set.

1 braid (12 to 14 servings)   *(see photo pages 22-23)*

Variation: Prune or Apricot Filling may be substituted to change Nut Braid into a Fruit Braid.

PRUNE NUT TWIST

1 recipe Basic Sweet Dough for
   Coffee Cakes (page 24)
1 can Solo or 1 jar Baker Prune
   Filling
¼ cup granulated sugar
1 teaspoon cinnamon

½ cup finely chopped walnuts or
   pecans
2 tablespoons orange-flavored
   brandy or orange juice
1 egg yolk beaten with 1 tablespoon
   milk for brushing

Glaze (optional):
1 cup confectioners sugar   1 to 2 tablespoons milk

Preheat oven to 375°F. Grease baking sheet and set aside.

Punch dough down and divide in half. Roll out 1 piece of dough to 10 x 16-inch rectangle. Combine prune filling, granulated sugar, cinnamon, nuts, and brandy in small bowl. Spread half of prune filling over dough to within ½ inch of edges all the way around. Roll dough tightly, jelly-roll style, starting from long side. Pinch seam to seal. Repeat with remaining dough and prune filling.

Place filled rolls next to each other on prepared baking sheet and pinch top ends together. Twist rolls and shape twist into ring. Pinch ends together. Cut ½-inch-deep slashes about 1½ inches apart all the way around outside of ring. Brush with beaten egg yolk mixture.

Bake 30 to 35 minutes or until deep golden brown. Remove from baking sheet and cool completely on wire rack.

To make glaze, combine confectioners sugar and milk in small bowl and stir until smooth. Spoon or drizzle glaze over cooled coffee cake. Let stand until glaze is set.

1 coffee cake (10 to 12 servings)

TRADITIONAL ALMOND KRINGLE

1 package active dry yeast
¼ cup warm water (105°F-115°F)
4 cups all-purpose flour
2 tablespoons granulated sugar
1 teaspoon salt

1 cup butter or margarine, softened
2 eggs
¾ cup milk
1 can Solo or 1 jar Baker Almond
   Filling

Brown Butter Icing:

⅓ cup butter or margarine
3 cups sifted confectioners sugar
3 tablespoons light cream
¼ teaspoon almond extract

Toasted sliced almonds and
   chopped maraschino cherries to
   decorate (optional)

Sprinkle yeast over warm water and stir to dissolve. Let stand 5 to 10 minutes or until foamy. Combine flour, granulated sugar, and salt in large bowl and stir until blended. Cut in butter until mixture resembles coarse crumbs. Beat eggs and milk until blended. Add to dry ingredients with yeast mixture and stir just until all particles are moistened. (Dough will be sticky.) Cover bowl with plastic wrap and overwrap with aluminum foil. Refrigerate 4 hours or overnight. (Dough will rise very slightly.)

Grease 2 baking sheets and set aside.

Remove dough from refrigerator and divide in half. Sprinkle 1 piece of dough with flour and knead gently 10 to 12 strokes on lightly floured surface. Roll out to 18 x 12-inch rectangle. Spread half of almond filling in 3-inch strip lengthwise down center of dough. Fold 1 long side of dough over filling and fold other side over. Pinch edge and ends to seal.

Place, seam side down, on prepared baking sheet and curve to make horseshoe shape. Repeat with remaining dough and almond filling. Cover with towels and set aside in warm, draft-free place to rise until light, about 30 minutes.

Preheat oven to 375°F.

Bake 20 to 25 minutes or until golden brown. Remove from baking sheets and cool on wire racks.

To make icing, place butter in medium-size saucepan and cook over medium heat until nut brown in color. Remove from heat and beat in confectioners sugar and cream gradually until blended and smooth. Stir in almond extract. Frost warm Kringles and decorate with toasted sliced almonds and cherries, if desired.

2 coffee cakes (10 to 12 servings each)

Variation: Dust Kringles with confectioners sugar instead of using icing.

NUT-FILLED COFFEE CAKE

½ recipe Refrigerator Dough
(page 25)
1 can Solo or 1 jar Baker Nut Filling
½ cup chopped maraschino cherries

1 egg beaten with 1 tablespoon milk
for brushing
Confectioners sugar

Grease baking sheet and set aside.

Roll out dough on lightly floured surface to 10 x 14-inch rectangle. Spread nut filling over dough to within ½ inch of edges all the way around and sprinkle chopped cherries over filling. Roll up dough, jelly-roll style, starting from long side. Pinch seam to seal. Place, seam side down, on prepared baking sheet and pinch and tuck ends under. Cut slashes, about 1½ inches apart, across top of filled roll. Cover with greased waxed paper and cover waxed paper lightly with plastic wrap. Let rise in refrigerator 2 to 24 hours.

Remove coffee cake from refrigerator, uncover, and let stand at room temperature 15 minutes. Preheat oven to 375°F. Brush coffee cake with beaten egg mixture.

Bake 25 to 30 minutes or until deep golden brown. Remove from baking sheet and cool completely on wire rack. Dust with confectioners sugar before serving.

1 coffee cake (8 to 10 servings)

APPLE CARAMEL STICKY BUNS

½ cup butter or margarine, melted
½ cup firmly packed brown sugar
2 tablespoons light corn syrup
½ cup chopped pecans
1 recipe Basic Sweet Dough for
Coffee Cakes (page 24)

1 can Solo or 1 jar Baker Apple
Filling
½ cup raisins
½ teaspoon cinnamon

Grease 9 x 13-inch baking pan. Combine butter, brown sugar, corn syrup, and pecans. Spread evenly in bottom of prepared pan and set aside.

Punch dough down and roll out dough on lightly floured surface to 12 x 16-inch rectangle. Spread apple filling over dough to within ½ inch of edges all the way around. Sprinkle raisins and cinnamon over filling.

Roll up dough, jelly-roll style, starting from long side. Pinch seam to seal. Cut filled dough into 15 slices with very sharp knife. Arrange slices, cut side down, in prepared pan. Space slices evenly, leaving enough space between slices to allow for expansion. Cover with towel and set aside in warm, draft-free place to rise until doubled in bulk, about 45 minutes.

Preheat oven to 375°F. Bake 30 to 35 minutes or until golden brown. Invert pan carefully onto large, flat platter or baking sheet. Remove pan and let cool. Serve warm.

15 buns

ALMOND STAR RING

½ recipe Refrigerator Dough
  (page 25)
1 can Solo or 1 jar Baker Almond
  Filling

1 teaspoon cinnamon
1 egg beaten with 1 tablespoon milk
  for brushing

Glaze:

1 cup confectioners sugar

1 to 2 tablespoons milk or water

Grease baking sheet and set aside.

Roll out dough on lightly floured surface to 14 x 16-inch rectangle. Spread filling over dough to within ½ inch of edges all the way around. Sprinkle with cinnamon and roll up dough, jelly-roll style, starting from long side. Pinch seam to seal. Place on prepared baking sheet and shape into ring, pinching ends together to seal.

Cut 8 connected "Vs" (16 connected diagonal lines) around outside curve of ring to create 8-point star. Cover with greased waxed paper and cover waxed paper lightly with plastic wrap. Let rise in refrigerator 2 to 24 hours.

Preheat oven to 375°F.

Uncover ring and let stand at room temperature 15 minutes. Brush with beaten egg mixture. Bake 25 to 30 minutes or until deep golden brown. Remove from baking sheet and cool completely on wire rack.

To make glaze, combine sugar and milk in small bowl and stir until smooth. Drizzle over cooled coffee cake. Let stand until glaze is set.

1 coffee ring (10 to 12 servings)

Use single-edge razor to cut 8 connected "Vs" around outside of ring.

YEAST KOLACKY

About 3½ cups all-purpose flour
¼ cup sugar
1 package active dry yeast
1 teaspoon salt
¼ cup butter or margarine
1 cup milk
3 egg yolks

1 teaspoon mace
1 teaspoon grated lemon peel
4 tablespoons unsalted butter,
    melted and cooled for brushing
1 can Solo or 1 jar Baker Filling
    (any flavor)

Combine 1½ cups flour, sugar, yeast, and salt in large bowl and stir until blended. Place ¼ cup butter and milk in small saucepan. Cook over low heat until very warm (120°F-130°F). Add to dry ingredients gradually, beating with electric mixer at low speed until blended. Increase speed to medium and beat 2 minutes. Add egg yolks, ½ cup flour, mace, and lemon peel. Beat 2 minutes. Stir in enough remaining flour to make stiff dough. Turn out onto lightly floured surface and knead until smooth and elastic, 5 to 8 minutes.

Place dough in greased bowl and turn to coat entire surface of dough. Cover with towel and set aside in warm, draft-free place to rise until doubled in bulk, about 1 hour.

Grease baking sheets and set aside.

Punch dough down and divide into 4 equal-size pieces. Cut each piece into 9 equal-size pieces. Shape each piece into small ball, pinching and tucking ends under. Place balls, smooth side up, on prepared baking sheets about 2 inches apart. Brush balls with 2 tablespoons melted butter. Set aside in warm, draft-free place to rise until doubled in bulk, about 45 minutes.

Preheat oven to 400°F.

Press center of each ball with thumb to make deep depression. Fill depression with desired filling. Let rise 10 to 12 minutes.

Bake 12 to 15 minutes or until golden brown. Brush kolacky with remaining 2 tablespoons melted butter as soon as they are removed from oven. Remove from baking sheets and cool completely on wire racks.

36 kolacky

POPPY CROWN COFFEE CAKE

About 3½ cups all-purpose flour
¼ cup sugar
½ teaspoon salt
1 package active dry yeast
1¼ cups milk
½ cup butter or margarine

2 eggs, beaten
1 can Solo or 1 jar Baker Poppy
  Filling
½ cup raisins
1 tablespoon grated orange peel
Confectioners sugar

Combine 1½ cups flour, sugar, salt, and yeast in large bowl and stir until blended. Place milk and butter in small saucepan. Cook over low heat until very warm (120°F-130°F). Add to dry ingredients gradually and beat with electric mixer at low speed until blended. Increase speed to medium and beat 2 minutes. Beat in eggs and 1 cup flour. Beat 2 minutes. Stir in enough remaining flour to make stiff dough. Turn out onto lightly floured surface and knead until smooth and elastic, 5 to 8 minutes.

Place in greased bowl and turn to coat entire surface of dough. Cover with clean towel and set aside in warm, draft-free place to rise until doubled in bulk, about 1 hour.

Grease 10-cup kugelhopf pan or 12-cup Bundt pan and set aside.

Punch dough down. Roll out on lightly floured surface to 8 x 15-inch rectangle. Spread poppy filling over dough to within ½ inch of edge all the way around. Sprinkle raisins and orange peel over poppy filling. Roll up dough, jelly-roll style, starting from long side. Pinch seam and ends to seal. Place, seam side down, in prepared pan and tuck ends under. Cover with towel and set aside in warm, draft-free place to rise until doubled in bulk, about 45 minutes.

Preheat oven to 325°F.

Bake 1 hour or until top is golden brown. Remove from pan and cool completely on wire rack. Dust with confectioners sugar before serving.

1 coffee cake (8 to 12 servings)

SOUR CREAM POPPY CRESCENTS

About 4½ cups all-purpose flour
¼ cup granulated sugar
1 package active dry yeast
1 teaspoon salt
1 cup butter or margarine
1 cup dairy sour cream

¼ cup water
2 egg yolks
1 teaspoon vanilla
1 can Solo or 1 jar Baker Poppy
  Filling

Sugar Glaze:
1 cup confectioners sugar
½ teaspoon vanilla

1½ to 2 tablespoons milk or water

Combine 1½ cups flour, granulated sugar, yeast, and salt in large bowl, and stir until blended. Place butter, sour cream, and water in small saucepan. Cook over low heat until very warm (120°F-130°F). Add to dry ingredients gradually and beat with electric mixer at low speed until blended. Increase speed to medium and beat 2 minutes. Add egg yolks and vanilla and beat 1 minute. Stir in enough remaining flour to make stiff dough. Turn out on lightly floured surface and knead until smooth and elastic, 5 to 8 minutes.

Place dough in greased bowl and turn to coat entire surface of dough. Cover with towel and set aside in warm, draft-free place to rise until doubled in bulk, about 1 hour.

Preheat oven to 375°F. Grease 2 large baking sheets and set aside.

Punch dough down and divide into 5 equal-size pieces. Roll out 1 piece of dough on lightly floured surface to 10-inch circle. Spread one-fifth of poppy filling on circle. Cut circle into 6 equal-size pie-shape wedges. Roll up wedges, jelly-roll style, starting from wide end. Place filled crescents, pointed end down, on prepared baking sheets 2 to 3 inches apart and curve ends to form crescents. Repeat with remaining dough and poppy filling.

Bake 20 to 25 minutes or until golden brown. Remove from baking sheets and cool on wire racks.

To make glaze, combine confectioners sugar, vanilla, and milk in small bowl, and stir until smooth. Drizzle glaze over warm crescents and let stand until glaze is set.

30 crescents

BOHEMIAN FRUIT SLICES

2 cups all-purpose flour	**¼ cup warm water (105°F-115°F)**
⅓ cup sugar	**1 egg, lightly beaten**
½ teaspoon salt	**1 can Solo or 1 jar Baker Prune or**
¾ cup butter or margarine, softened	**Date Filling**
1 package active dry yeast	**Confectioners sugar**

Preheat oven to 375°F. Grease large baking sheet and set aside.

Combine flour, sugar, and salt in medium-size bowl and stir until blended. Cut in butter until mixture resembles coarse crumbs.

Sprinkle yeast over warm water and stir to dissolve. Let stand 5 to 10 minutes or until foamy. Add yeast mixture and beaten egg to flour mixture and mix until dough binds together and comes away from side of bowl.

Dust hands with flour and shape dough into ball. Divide dough in half. Roll out 1 piece of dough on well-floured surface to 13 x 9-inch rectangle. Spread half of prune filling over dough to within ½ inch of edges all the way around. Roll up dough, jelly-roll style, starting from long side. Pinch seam and ends to seal. Place, seam side down, on prepared baking sheet. Repeat with remaining dough and filling. Make ½-inch-deep slash lengthwise down center of rolls.

Bake 25 to 28 minutes or until golden brown. Remove from baking sheet and cool on wire rack. Dust rolls with confectioners sugar while still warm. When cool, cut into ¾-inch-thick diagonal slices.

About 34 slices

DANISH PASTRIES

1¼ cups unsalted butter, divided
    About 4 cups all-purpose flour
⅓ cup sugar
2 packages active dry yeast
1 teaspoon salt
1 cup milk

2 eggs
1 can Solo or 1 jar Baker Filling
    (any flavor)
1 egg beaten with 1 tablespoon water
    for brushing
Confectioners sugar

Place 1 cup butter between two large sheets of waxed paper and roll out to 6 x 12-inch rectangle. Refrigerate until firm, about 1 hour.

Combine 1½ cups flour, sugar, yeast, and salt in large bowl, and stir until blended. Place remaining ¼ cup butter and milk in small saucepan. Cook over low heat until very warm (120°F-130°F). Add to dry ingredients gradually, beating with electric mixer at low speed until blended. Increase speed to medium and beat 2 minutes. Add eggs and 1 cup flour and beat 2 minutes. Stir in enough remaining flour to make stiff dough. Turn out onto lightly floured surface and knead until smooth and elastic, 5 to 8 minutes.

Shape dough into slightly flattened ball, cover with towel, and let rest on lightly floured surface 30 minutes.

Roll out dough on lightly floured surface to 15-inch square. Remove butter from refrigerator and peel off top sheet of waxed paper. Invert butter over half of dough and remove waxed paper. Fold unbuttered portion of dough over buttered dough. Press edges down firmly to seal. Roll out to 12 x 20-inch rectangle and fold dough in thirds, envelope style. Wrap in waxed paper or plastic wrap and refrigerate 30 minutes.

Unwrap dough and roll out on lightly floured surface to 12 x 20-inch rectangle. Fold in thirds. Wrap and refrigerate 30 minutes. Repeat rolling, folding, and refrigerating twice, refrigerating 30 minutes after last rolling.

To shape pastries, cut dough into 4 equal-size pieces. Wrap 3 pieces and return to refrigerator. Roll out 1 piece of dough to 8 x 12-inch rectangle and cut into six 4-inch squares. Spoon about 1 tablespoon filling onto center of each square. Brush pastry edges with beaten egg mixture. Repeat with remaining dough and filling.

To make envelopes, bring 4 corners of dough to center to enclose filling. Pinch edges lightly to seal.

To make pinwheels, cut squares diagonally from corners partway in toward center. Fold every other point in to center to enclose filling and press lightly to secure.

To make bear claws, fold squares in half. Cut 3 or 4 slashes along folded edge about three-quarters of the way in. Spread slashes slightly apart to make bear claws.

Place filled pastries on ungreased baking sheets about 2 inches apart. Cover loosely and set aside in warm, draft-free place to rise until almost doubled and puffed, 30 to 45 minutes. Preheat oven to 425°F.

Brush pastries with beaten egg mixture and bake 10 to 12 minutes or until golden brown. Remove from baking sheets and cool completely on wire racks. Dust with confectioners sugar just before serving.

24 pastries

1: *Place butter over half the dough.*

2: *Fold unbuttered half over. Press edges to seal.*

3: *Roll out dough to 12" x 20" rectangle and fold dough in thirds, envelope style.*

4: *To make pinwheels, fold every other point in to center.*

PINEAPPLE KUCHEN

1 package active dry yeast
¼ cup warm water (105°F-115°F)
¼ cup butter or margarine, melted
    and cooled
¼ cup milk

2 cups all-purpose flour
2 tablespoons sugar
¼ teaspoon salt
1 egg, beaten

Topping:

1 package (8 ounces) cream cheese,
    softened
¼ cup sugar

1 egg
1 can Solo or 1 jar Baker Pineapple
    Filling or any flavor Fruit Filling

Sprinkle yeast over warm water in medium-size bowl. Stir to dissolve. Let stand 5 to 10 minutes or until foamy. Add melted butter and milk and stir to blend. Stir in 1 cup flour, sugar, and salt. Add beaten egg and remaining 1 cup flour, ½ cup at a time. Stir to make stiff dough that comes away from side of bowl. Turn out onto lightly floured surface and knead until smooth and elastic, about 5 to 8 minutes.

Place in greased bowl and turn to coat entire surface of dough. Cover with clean towel and set aside in warm, draft-free place to rise until doubled in bulk, about 1 hour.

Grease 15 x 10-inch jelly-roll pan and set aside.

Punch dough down. Roll out on lightly floured surface to 15 x 10-inch rectangle and pat evenly in prepared pan, building edge up slightly all the way around.

To make topping, beat cream cheese, sugar, and egg in medium-size bowl until blended and smooth. Spread cream cheese mixture over dough. Spoon pineapple filling over cream cheese mixture and spread lightly with back of spoon. Let rise, uncovered, in warm, draft-free place 35 minutes.

Preheat oven to 325°F.

Bake 20 to 25 minutes or until edge of dough is golden brown. Cool completely in pan on wire rack.

15 servings

APPLE RAISIN PLAIT

About 2½ cups all-purpose flour
1 package active dry yeast
3 tablespoons sugar
1 teaspoon salt
1 teaspoon grated lemon peel
½ cup milk
3 tablespoons butter or margarine

1 egg
1 can Solo or 1 jar Baker Apple
Filling
½ cup raisins
1 teaspoon cinnamon
1 egg beaten with 1 tablespoon milk
for brushing

Combine 1 cup flour, yeast, sugar, salt, and lemon peel in medium-size bowl, and stir until blended. Place milk and butter in small saucepan. Cook over low heat until very warm (120°F-130°F). Add to dry ingredients gradually and beat with electric mixer at low speed until blended. Increase speed to medium and beat 2 minutes. Beat in egg. Stir in enough remaining flour to make stiff dough.

Turn out onto lightly floured surface and knead until smooth and elastic, 5 to 8 minutes. Place dough in greased bowl and turn to coat entire surface of dough. Cover with towel and set aside in warm, draft-free place to rise until doubled in bulk, about 1 hour.

Grease baking sheet. Punch dough down. Roll out on lightly floured surface to 12 x 16-inch rectangle and place on prepared baking sheet.

Combine apple filling, raisins, and cinnamon in small bowl. Spread apple mixture down center of dough in 3-inch-wide strip. Make diagonal cuts 1 inch apart down each side of dough from edge of plait in toward center almost to filling. Fold alternate right and left strips of dough over filling. Tuck and pinch ends under. Cover and let rise until almost doubled, about 45 minutes.

Preheat oven to 375°F.

Brush plait with beaten egg mixture. Bake 20 to 25 minutes or until deep golden brown. Remove from baking sheet and cool completely on wire rack.

1 plait (10 to 12 servings)

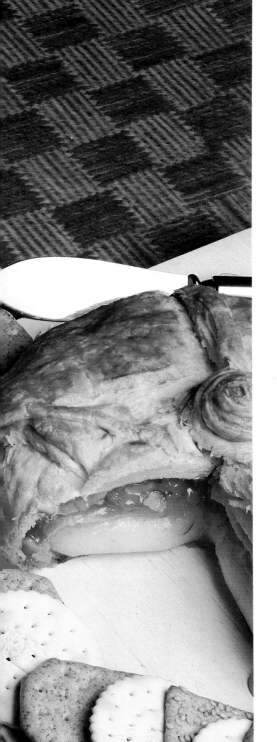

CHAPTER 3

*Appetizers,
Main Dishes,
and
Salads*

*Harvest Fruit Salad (page 41),
Apricot Brie in Puff Pastry
(page 40), Apple-Stuffed Pork
Roast (page 49)*

Quick APRICOT BACON APPETIZERS

1 pound thick-sliced bacon	2 tablespoons Dijon-style mustard
1 can Solo or 1 jar Baker Apricot or Pineapple Filling	1 tablespoon soy sauce

Preheat oven to 400°F. Line 15 x 10-inch jelly-roll pan with aluminum foil. Place large wire rack in foil-lined pan.

Cut bacon slices in half crosswise and arrange on rack in single layer. Combine apricot filling, mustard, and soy sauce in small bowl and stir until blended. Spread half of apricot mixture over bacon.

Bake 15 minutes. Turn bacon over with tongs and spread remaining apricot mixture over. Bake 5 minutes or until bacon is crisp. Let stand on rack in pan 5 minutes before removing.

10 to 12 servings

Microwave Method: Arrange one-fourth of bacon slices on microproof rack. Prepare apricot mixture as directed above and spread one-eighth of mixture over bacon. Cover loosely with waxed paper. Microcook on high (100%) power 3½ minutes. Turn bacon over and spread one-eighth of apricot mixture over. Cover and microcook on high (100%) power 1 minute. Let stand 1 minute. Remove from rack and place on serving plate. Drain fat from rack and repeat with remaining bacon and apricot mixture.

Easy APRICOT BRIE IN PUFF PASTRY

1 sheet (½ of 17¼-ounce package) frozen puff pastry, thawed	½ cup sliced almonds
1 wheel (17.6 ounces) baby Brie	1 egg beaten with 1 tablespoon water for brushing
1 can Solo or 1 jar Baker Apricot Filling	

Preheat oven to 375°F. Line baking sheet with parchment paper and set aside.

Unfold pastry and lay flat on lightly floured surface. Roll out to 14-inch square. Cut out 14-inch circle and reserve pastry trimmings. Place Brie in middle of pastry circle.

Spread apricot filling around side and over top of Brie. Sprinkle almonds over filling. Brush beaten egg mixture around pastry edge. Fold pastry up and over Brie, covering Brie completely. Press and pinch edges to seal. Lift Brie onto lined baking sheet with large spatula and brush pastry liberally all over with beaten egg mixture. Use pastry trimmings to make decorative cutouts, if desired. Arrange cutouts on pastry-wrapped Brie and brush with beaten egg mixture.

Bake 25 to 30 minutes or until pastry is puffed and golden brown. Remove from baking sheet with large spatula and cool on wire rack at least 45 minutes. Serve warm with assorted cocktail breads and crackers.

12 to 16 servings   *(see photo page 39)*

CABBAGE AND APPLE SLAW

1 can Solo or 1 jar Baker Apple
   Filling
¼ cup honey
3 tablespoons cider vinegar
1 tablespoon vegetable oil
½ teaspoon celery seed

4 cups shredded cabbage (about
   1 medium-size head)
1 cup shredded carrots (about
   2 large carrots)
⅓ to ½ cup raisins
Salt and freshly ground pepper
   to taste

Place apple filling, honey, vinegar, oil, and celery seed in small bowl and stir until thoroughly blended.

Place cabbage, carrots, and raisins in medium-size bowl. Add apple mixture and stir until well mixed. Season with salt and pepper. Cover and refrigerate 2 to 3 hours or until chilled.

6 to 8 servings

FRUITY COLESLAW

4 cups shredded cabbage (about 1
   medium-size head)
1 cup shredded carrots (about 2
   medium-size carrots)
1 small green pepper, seeded and
   chopped
1 stalk celery, chopped
1 small red onion, chopped
1 can (11 ounces) mandarin oranges,
   drained

1 small apple, coarsely chopped
1 can Solo or 1 jar Baker Pineapple
   Filling
¾ cup mayonnaise
2 tablespoons sugar
2 tablespoons white or cider vinegar
Salt and freshly ground pepper
   to taste

Place cabbage, carrots, green pepper, celery, onion, oranges, and apple in large bowl and toss until well mixed.

Place pineapple filling, mayonnaise, sugar, vinegar, salt, and pepper in medium-size bowl and stir until thoroughly blended. Spoon over vegetables and toss to coat. Cover and refrigerate 3 to 4 hours or until chilled.

6 to 8 servings

Quick HARVEST FRUIT SALAD

2 cups fresh cranberries, coarsely
   chopped
1 cup chopped pecans

2 cans (15 ounces each) fruit
   cocktail, drained
1 cup Solo Fruit Salad Dressing

Combine cranberries, pecans, and fruit cocktail in medium-size bowl. Add fruit salad dressing and toss gently. Refrigerate 2 to 3 hours or until ready to serve.

6 to 8 servings *(see photo page 38)*

Quick PINEAPPLE WALDORF SALAD

1 can Solo or 1 jar Baker Pineapple
  or Apricot Filling
½ cup mayonnaise
6 medium-size unpeeled red apples,
  cored and cut into 1-inch cubes

3 stalks celery, sliced
½ cup chopped pecans, toasted if
  desired
Lettuce leaves to serve

Combine pineapple filling and mayonnaise in small bowl and set aside.

Place apples, celery, and pecans in large bowl and toss gently to mix. Add pineapple mixture and stir well. Cover and refrigerate 2 to 3 hours or until chilled. Serve on bed of lettuce.

6 servings

Easy ORANGE AVOCADO SALAD

3 large navel oranges, peeled, pith
  removed, and coarsely chopped
1 large ripe avocado, peeled and
  chopped
4 to 6 red onion slices, separated
  into rings

1 head Bibb lettuce, torn into
  bite-size pieces
2 tablespoons cider vinegar
1 tablespoon soy sauce
4 tablespoons Solo Fruit Salad
  Dressing
Alfalfa sprouts to garnish

Place chopped oranges, avocado, onion rings, and lettuce in large bowl and toss gently. Stir vinegar and soy sauce into fruit salad dressing. Pour over salad and toss gently. Top each serving with alfalfa sprouts and serve immediately.

4 servings

Easy APRICOT CARROT SALAD

1 can Solo or 1 jar Baker Apricot
  Filling
¼ cup mayonnaise
½ cup raisins

3 cups shredded carrots (about 6
  medium-size carrots)
1 can (11 ounces) mandarin oranges,
  drained
Lettuce leaves to serve

Place apricot filling, mayonnaise, and raisins in medium-size bowl and stir until well mixed. Add carrots and mandarin oranges and stir. Cover and refrigerate 2 to 3 hours or until chilled. Serve on bed of lettuce.

4 to 6 servings

Easy

TURKEY BREAST WITH CHERRY STUFFING

1 fresh turkey breast (about 5 pounds), boned
1 can Solo or 1 jar Baker Cherry Filling
1½ cups herb-seasoned stuffing mix
½ cup chopped pecans
½ teaspoon grated lemon peel
Salt to taste
2 to 3 tablespoons butter or margarine, melted
Paprika

Preheat oven to 325°F.

Rinse turkey breast under cold running water and pat dry. Combine cherry filling, stuffing mix, pecans, lemon peel, and salt in medium-size bowl and stir until well blended. Place turkey breast, skin side down, on work surface and cut deep slit lengthwise down center of breast. Season with salt and spoon cherry stuffing into slit. Tie meat securely in several places with kitchen string to close over filling. Place on rack in shallow roasting pan. Brush turkey with melted butter and sprinkle with paprika.

Roast 2 hours to 2 hours 15 minutes or until temperature registers 170°F on meat thermometer, brushing with pan juices several times during cooking. Let stand 15 minutes before carving.

10 to 12 servings

Microwave Method: Prepare turkey breast and stuffing as directed above. Place stuffed turkey breast, skin side down, on microproof rack in microproof baking dish. Brush with half of melted butter and sprinkle with paprika. Microcook on high (100%) power 25 minutes. Turn skin side up, brush with remaining butter, and sprinkle with paprika. Microcook on medium (50%) power 30 to 35 minutes or until temperature registers 170°F on instant meat thermometer. Let stand 15 minutes before carving.

Easy
TART RED CABBAGE AND APPLES

¼ cup butter or margarine
2 cups shredded red cabbage
  (about 1 small head)
1 small onion, chopped
¼ cup chicken broth or chicken
  bouillon

1 can Solo or 1 jar Baker Apple
  Filling
¼ cup cider vinegar
¼ teaspoon ground cloves
Salt and freshly ground pepper
  to taste

Melt butter in large saucepan or Dutch oven. Add cabbage, onion, and broth, and cook until cabbage is tender.

Add apple filling, vinegar, cloves, salt, and pepper and stir until well mixed. Cover and cook over low heat until heated through, stirring occasionally.

4 servings

Microwave Method: Place butter in 2-quart microproof casserole and micro-cook on high (100%) power 1½ minutes or until melted. Add cabbage, onion, and broth, and stir well. Cover and microcook on high (100%) power 10 to 12 minutes or until cabbage is tender, stirring after 5 minutes. Drain off excess liquid. Stir in apple filling, vinegar, cloves, salt, and pepper. Cover and microcook on high (100%) power 3 to 4 minutes or until heated through, stirring after 2 minutes.

Quick
APPLE-FILLED SQUASH

2 acorn squash (about 1 pound each)
4 teaspoons butter or margarine,
  melted

1 can Solo or 1 jar Baker Apple
  Filling
½ teaspoon allspice or pumpkin
  pie spice

Preheat oven to 350°F.

Cut squash in half and scoop out seeds. Place, cut side up, in baking dish and brush cavities with melted butter. Bake 45 minutes or until fork tender. Spoon apple filling into cavities and sprinkle with allspice. Bake 15 minutes or until filling is hot and bubbly.

4 servings

Microwave Method: Pierce skin of whole squash in several places with long-tined fork. Place in microproof dish and microcook on high (100%) power 10 to 14 minutes or until fork tender. Cut squash in half and scoop out seeds. Place, cut side up, in microproof dish and brush with melted butter. Fill as directed above and cover loosely with waxed paper. Cook on high (100%) power 4 to 6 minutes or until filling is hot and bubbly.

Easy   FRUITY APPLE YAM PUFFS

2 cans (16 ounces each) yams or
  sweet potatoes, well drained
1 can Solo or 1 jar Baker Apple or
  Pineapple Filling
¼ cup all-purpose flour

1 teaspoon cinnamon
¼ teaspoon nutmeg
⅛ teaspoon ground cloves
4 cups corn flakes, crushed

Preheat oven to 375°F. Grease 2 baking sheets and set aside.

Place yams in container of food processor and process until puréed, or mash in bowl with potato masher.

Spoon puréed yams into medium-size bowl. Add apple filling and stir until combined. Stir flour, cinnamon, nutmeg, and cloves, and fold into yam mixture.

Place corn flake crumbs in shallow bowl. Drop yam mixture into crumbs, 1 tablespoonful at a time, and turn to coat all sides. Shape into balls and place on prepared baking sheets.

Bake 20 to 25 minutes or until deep golden brown. Remove from baking sheets and place on serving plate. Serve warm with baked Virginia ham, roast pork, or turkey.

36 to 40 puffs

PINEAPPLE-GLAZED CARROTS

2 pounds carrots
3 tablespoons butter or margarine
1 can Solo or 1 jar Baker Pineapple
  Filling
2 tablespoons brown sugar
2 tablespoons lemon juice

1 to 2 teaspoons grated orange or
  lemon peel
¼ teaspoon cinnamon
Salt and freshly ground pepper
  to taste

Peel carrots and cut into 1½-inch sticks. Bring large saucepan of lightly salted water to a boil. Add carrots and cook just until tender. Drain, reserving 3 tablespoons cooking liquid. Set carrots aside.

Wipe saucepan with paper towel. Melt butter in saucepan. Stir in pineapple filling. Add brown sugar, lemon juice, orange peel, cinnamon, and reserved cooking liquid. Stir until blended. Simmer 2 minutes. Add carrots, season with salt and pepper, and stir gently to coat. Cook just until heated through. Serve immediately.

6 to 8 servings

SPICY CHERRY CHICKEN WINGS

14 to 18 chicken wings (tips removed)
¾ cup all-purpose flour
1 teaspoon garlic powder
1 teaspoon paprika
½ teaspoon thyme
   Salt and freshly ground pepper
     to taste
1 egg beaten with 1 tablespoon water
   Vegetable oil for deep-fat frying

1 can Solo or 1 jar Baker Cherry
   Filling
2 to 3 tablespoons Dijon-style
   mustard
¼ teaspoon cayenne
¼ cup orange juice
2 tablespoons lemon juice
1 tablespoon cider vinegar
   Toasted sesame seed (optional)

Cut each chicken wing through joint to make 2 pieces. Combine flour, garlic powder, paprika, thyme, salt, and pepper in plastic bag. Dip a few chicken pieces in beaten egg, shake off excess egg, and place in plastic bag. Shake to coat thoroughly and place on sheet of waxed paper. Repeat with remaining chicken.

Heat oil in deep-fat fryer. Deep-fry chicken, a few pieces at a time, until golden brown. Remove with slotted spoon, drain on paper towels, and place in deep bowl.

Stir cherry filling, mustard, cayenne, orange juice, lemon juice, and vinegar in small saucepan. Place over low heat and cook, stirring, just until heated through. Pour cherry sauce over chicken wings and toss gently to coat. Arrange on serving platter and sprinkle with sesame seed, if desired.

12 to 14 servings as appetizer
4 to 5 servings as main dish

Easy   SWEET AND SOUR SHRIMP

1 pound medium-size shrimp
1 can Solo or 1 jar Baker Pineapple
   Filling
¼ cup cider vinegar
3 tablespoons soy sauce
2 tablespoons lemon juice
2 tablespoons brown sugar
½ teaspoon ground ginger

1 teaspoon prepared hot mustard,
   Chinese-style preferred (optional)
1 medium-size onion, sliced
1 medium-size green bell pepper,
   seeded and cut into chunks
1 medium-size red bell pepper,
   seeded and cut into chunks
   Hot cooked rice to serve

Shell and devein shrimp and set aside.

Combine pineapple filling, vinegar, soy sauce, lemon juice, brown sugar, ginger, and mustard in medium-size bowl and stir until thoroughly blended. Pour into 10-inch skillet and place over medium heat. Bring just to boiling point, reduce heat, add onion and green and red peppers, and cook 2 to 3 minutes. Add shrimp and cook 4 to 5 minutes or until shrimp turn pink, stirring occasionally. Serve immediately over hot cooked rice.

4 servings

Spicy Cherry Chicken Wings, Sweet and Sour Shrimp (opposite)

Quick   PEACH-GLAZED BEETS

2 cans (16 ounces each) sliced beets
1 jar Solo Peach Glaze
¼ cup cider vinegar

1½ tablespoons prepared horseradish
Salt and white pepper to taste

Drain beets, reserving 3 tablespoons liquid. Combine peach glaze, vinegar, horseradish, and reserved beet liquid in medium-size saucepan. Stir to blend. Add beets and stir gently to coat. Season with salt and pepper. Cook over low heat 8 to 10 minutes or until heated through, stirring occasionally. Serve immediately.

8 to 10 servings

Microwave Method: Drain beets, reserving 3 tablespoons liquid. Combine peach glaze, vinegar, horseradish, and reserved beet liquid in 2-quart microproof casserole. Stir to blend. Add beets and stir gently to coat. Season with salt and pepper. Cover with casserole cover or vented plastic wrap and microcook on medium-high (75%) power 5 to 6 minutes or until heated through, stirring once. Serve immediately.

Easy APRICOT ORANGE PORK CHOPS

2 tablespoons vegetable oil
6 center cut pork chops, trimmed of
    all visible fat
1 small orange, unpeeled, pits
    removed, and chopped
¼ cup dry white wine

2 tablespoons lemon juice
2 tablespoons brown sugar
1 can Solo or 1 jar Baker Apricot
    Filling
Hot cooked noodles to serve

Heat oil in large skillet. Add pork chops and cook until browned on both sides. Remove chops from skillet and place in single layer in shallow baking pan.

Preheat oven to 350°F.

Combine orange, wine, lemon juice, brown sugar, and apricot filling in small bowl and stir until blended. Spoon half of apricot orange mixture over chops.

Cover baking pan and bake 25 minutes. Uncover, turn chops over, and spoon remaining apricot orange mixture over chops. Bake 25 to 30 minutes or until chops are tender, adding a little water to pan if sauce is too thick. Serve immediately with hot cooked noodles.

6 servings

Easy APPLE-STUFFED PORK ROAST

1 can Solo or 1 jar Baker Apple
    Filling
⅓ cup golden raisins
4- to 5-pound center cut pork loin
    roast, bone-in

¾ cup orange juice
Watercress and crab apples
    for garnish (optional)

Preheat oven to 350°F.

Place apple filling and raisins in small bowl and stir. Make 2-inch-deep cut lengthwise down center of roast with sharp knife. Spoon half of apple mixture into opening. Tie roast in 3 or 4 places with kitchen string.

Place meat on rack in shallow baking pan. Bake 1 hour. Stir orange juice into remaining apple mixture and spoon over meat. Bake 1¼ to 1½ hours or until internal temperature registers 165°F on meat thermometer. Place on platter and garnish with watercress and crab apples, if desired. Let stand 10 minutes before carving.

6 servings   *(see photo page 38)*

APRICOT AND BRIE CHICKEN KIEV

1 cup seasoned dry bread crumbs
½ teaspoon garlic powder
Salt and freshly ground pepper
  to taste
4 large boned, skinned chicken
  breasts, cut in half

1 can Solo or 1 jar Baker Apricot
  Filling
8 tablespoons butter or margarine
8 ounces Brie, cut into 8 pieces
6 green onions, chopped
¼ cup freshly chopped parsley
2 eggs, beaten

Preheat oven to 375°F. Grease shallow baking pan.

Combine bread crumbs, garlic powder, salt, and pepper in shallow dish and stir until thoroughly blended. Set aside.

Pound breast halves between 2 pieces of waxed paper. Spread 2 tablespoons apricot filling on each breast half. Top with 1 tablespoon butter and 1 piece Brie. Sprinkle green onions and parsley over Brie.

Roll up chicken breast halves and secure with wooden toothpicks or small skewers. Dip in beaten eggs and roll in bread crumb mixture. Place in single layer in prepared pan.

Bake 25 to 30 minutes or until chicken is tender. Remove toothpicks before serving.

8 servings

BUFFET CHICKEN SALAD

5 cups cubed cooked chicken
  (5 whole boned, skinned chicken
  breasts)
4 cups seedless green grapes, halved
1 cup chopped celery
8 green onions, minced
3 cloves garlic, minced

Salt to taste
1 jar Solo Fruit Salad Dressing
2 tablespoons white vinegar
2 tablespoons soy sauce
½ teaspoon ground cloves
½ teaspoon ground coriander
1 cup toasted slivered almonds

Combine chicken, grapes, celery, green onions, garlic, and salt in large salad bowl.

Place fruit salad dressing in separate bowl. Add vinegar, soy sauce, cloves, and coriander and stir until blended. Add to chicken mixture and stir gently until well combined.

Cover and refrigerate 2 to 3 hours or until ready to serve. Stir in toasted almonds just before serving.

16 servings

SWEET AND PUNGENT PINEAPPLE RIBS

2 tablespoons vegetable oil
1 medium-size onion, chopped
1 clove garlic, minced
½ cup firmly packed brown sugar
1 can (8 ounces) tomato sauce
3 tablespoons cider vinegar
2 tablespoons Worcestershire sauce

1 teaspoon dry mustard
¼ teaspoon celery seed
Salt and freshly ground pepper
to taste
1 can Solo or 1 jar Baker Pineapple
Filling
4 pounds pork loin back ribs

Heat oil in medium-size saucepan. Add onion and sauté until onion is transparent. Add garlic and cook 2 to 3 minutes. Stir in brown sugar until dissolved. Add tomato sauce, vinegar, Worcestershire, mustard, celery seed, salt, and pepper, and stir. Cover and cook over medium heat 20 minutes or until sauce is thickened, stirring occasionally. Add pineapple filling and stir until thoroughly blended. Remove from heat and set aside.

Preheat oven to 350°F.

Place ribs in Dutch oven and cover with water. Cook over high heat until water comes to a boil. Reduce heat to low, cover, and simmer 5 minutes. Drain off water and place ribs on paper towels to drain.

Arrange ribs on rack in shallow baking pan and brush with half of sauce. Bake 30 minutes. Turn ribs over and baste with remaining sauce. Bake 30 minutes or until meat is tender and edges are browned. Cut into serving pieces.

4 servings

Variation: To make an appetizer instead of a main dish, substitute baby back ribs for loin back ribs. Prepare as directed above.

8 to 12 servings

CHAPTER 4

All Kinds of Cookies

Almond Chocolate Chip Cookies (page 54), Sour Cream Date Drops (page 54), Teatime Treats (page 68), Chocolate Peanut Brittle No-Bake Cookies (page 69)

ALMOND CHOCOLATE CHIP COOKIES

1 can Solo Almond Paste
1 cup butter or margarine, softened
½ cup granulated sugar
½ cup firmly packed brown sugar
2 eggs
½ teaspoon almond extract

2½ cups all-purpose flour
1 teaspoon baking soda
¼ teaspoon salt
1 package (12 ounces) semisweet
** chocolate morsels**
1 cup toasted slivered almonds

Preheat oven to 350°F. Grease 2 large baking sheets and set aside.

Break almond paste into small pieces and place in medium-size bowl or container of food processor. Add butter and beat with electric mixer or process until mixture is creamy and smooth. Add sugars, eggs, and almond extract, and beat or process until thoroughly blended. (If using food processor, transfer mixture to medium-size bowl.) Stir flour, baking soda, and salt until mixed. Add to almond mixture and stir until blended. Stir in chocolate and slivered almonds. Drop by heaping teaspoonfuls onto prepared baking sheets about 1½ inches apart.

Bake 12 to 15 minutes or until golden brown. Remove from baking sheets and cool on wire racks.

About 78 cookies   *(see photo pages 52-53)*

SOUR CREAM DATE DROPS

½ cup butter or margarine, softened
¾ cup firmly packed brown sugar
1 egg
1 teaspoon vanilla
1 can Solo or 1 jar Baker Date
** Filling**
2¼ cups all-purpose flour
½ teaspoon baking powder

½ teaspoon baking soda
½ teaspoon cinnamon
¼ teaspoon nutmeg
¼ teaspoon salt
½ cup dairy sour cream
2 cups quick-cooking rolled oats
About 54 walnut or pecan halves

Preheat oven to 375°F. Grease 2 baking sheets and set aside.

Beat butter and brown sugar in large bowl with electric mixer until light and fluffy. Add egg, vanilla, and date filling, and beat until blended. Stir flour, baking powder, baking soda, cinnamon, nutmeg, and salt until mixed. Add to date mixture and stir to blend. Stir in sour cream and oats until well mixed.

Drop mixture by rounded teaspoonfuls onto prepared baking sheets about 1 inch apart. Press walnut half onto center of each cookie.

Bake 14 to 16 minutes or until golden brown. Cool on baking sheets on wire racks 1 minute. Remove from baking sheets and cool completely on racks.

About 54 cookies   *(see photo pages 52-53)*

GRANOLA CRUNCH DROP COOKIES

1 cup butter or margarine, softened	**½ teaspoon salt**
½ cup granulated sugar	**1 can Solo Toasted Almond Crunch**
½ cup firmly packed brown sugar	**Topping**
2 eggs	**2 cups natural honey-almond**
1 teaspoon vanilla	**granola**
2 cups all-purpose flour	**3 cups crisp rice cereal squares,**
1 teaspoon baking soda	**lightly crushed**
½ teaspoon baking powder	

Preheat oven to 350°F. Grease 2 baking sheets and set aside.

Beat butter and sugars in large bowl with electric mixer until light and fluffy. Add eggs and vanilla and beat until blended. Stir in flour, baking soda, baking powder, and salt until mixed. Add toasted almond crunch topping, granola, and rice cereal, and stir until well mixed. Drop mixture by heaping teaspoonfuls onto prepared baking sheets about 1 inch apart.

Bake 10 to 12 minutes or until edges of cookies are golden brown. Remove from baking sheets and cool completely on wire racks.

About 72 cookies

Easy   OAT CRUNCH BARS

4 cups quick-cooking rolled oats	**½ cup wheat germ**
1 jar (8 ounces) dry-roasted peanuts,	**½ cup sunflower seed**
coarsely chopped	**1 teaspoon cinnamon**
1 can Solo Crunch Topping	**½ cup butter or margarine**
(any kind)	**1 cup honey**

Preheat oven to 325°F. Grease 15 x 10-inch jelly-roll pan and set aside.

Combine oats, peanuts, crunch topping, wheat germ, sunflower seed, and cinnamon in large bowl, and set aside.

Place butter and honey in medium-size saucepan. Cook until butter is melted and mixture comes to a boil, stirring occasionally. Add to oat mixture slowly, stirring with wooden spoon until mixture is well coated. Spoon into prepared pan and spread or pat down evenly with back of wooden spoon.

Bake 20 to 25 minutes or until top is golden brown. Cool in pan on wire rack 30 minutes. Cut into thirty 1½ x 3⅓-inch bars with very sharp knife.

30 bars

CHERRY CHEESECAKE BARS

1 cup all-purpose flour
½ cup firmly packed brown sugar
1 cup butter or margarine

1 cup shredded or flaked coconut
½ cup quick-cooking rolled oats
½ cup chopped pecans or walnuts

Topping:
2 packages (8 ounces each) cream
    cheese, softened
1 cup granulated sugar
4 eggs

2 teaspoons vanilla
½ teaspoon grated lemon peel
1 can Solo or 1 jar Baker Cherry
    Filling or any flavor Fruit Filling

Preheat oven to 350°F. Grease 13 x 9-inch baking pan and set aside.

Stir flour and brown sugar in medium-size bowl until blended. Cut in butter until mixture resembles coarse crumbs. Add coconut, oats, and pecans, and stir until well mixed. Press mixture evenly onto bottom of prepared pan.

Bake 20 minutes or until crust is lightly browned. Cool in pan on wire rack 10 minutes.

To make topping, beat cream cheese, granulated sugar, eggs, vanilla, and lemon peel in medium-size bowl with electric mixer until blended and smooth. Pour over crust and spread evenly.

Bake 40 to 45 minutes or until center is set. Cool completely in pan on wire rack. Spread cherry filling over cooled cheesecake. Cover pan and refrigerate 2 to 3 hours or until well chilled. Cut into eighteen 2⅛ x 3-inch bars.

18 bars

DOUBLE CHOCOLATE RASPBERRY BARS

1¾ cups all-purpose flour
¼ cup unsweetened cocoa powder
1 cup granulated sugar
1 cup butter or margarine
1 egg, lightly beaten
1 teaspoon vanilla

1 can Solo or 1 jar Baker Raspberry
   Filling
1 cup chopped almonds or pecans
6 squares (6 ounces) semisweet
   chocolate, finely chopped, or
1 package (6 ounces) semisweet
   chocolate morsels

Glaze:

1 cup confectioners sugar

1 to 2 tablespoons milk

Preheat oven to 350°F. Grease 13 x 9-inch baking pan and set aside.

Stir flour, cocoa powder, and granulated sugar in medium-size bowl until blended. Cut in butter until mixture resembles coarse crumbs. Add egg and vanilla and stir until dry ingredients are thoroughly moistened. Measure 1 cup mixture and set aside. Press remaining mixture evenly into bottom of prepared pan. Cover with raspberry filling, spreading evenly.

Combine reserved 1 cup mixture, chopped almonds, and chopped chocolate. Sprinkle over raspberry filling.

Bake 40 minutes. Cool completely in pan on wire rack.

To make glaze, combine confectioners sugar and milk in small bowl and stir until smooth. Drizzle glaze in zig-zag pattern over cooled bars. Let stand until glaze is set. Cut into forty-eight 1½ x 1⅝-inch bars.

48 bars

CRUNCHY BROWNIES

½ cup butter or margarine, softened
1 cup sugar
2 eggs
1 teaspoon vanilla
¾ cup all-purpose flour
⅓ cup unsweetened cocoa powder

½ teaspoon baking powder
¼ teaspoon salt
½ cup Solo Peanut Brittle Crunch
   Topping
½ cup semisweet chocolate morsels

Preheat oven to 350°F. Grease 8-inch square baking pan and set aside.

Beat butter and sugar in medium-size bowl with electric mixer until light and fluffy. Add eggs and vanilla and beat until blended. Stir flour, cocoa powder, baking powder, and salt until mixed. Add to butter mixture and stir until blended and smooth. Spread batter evenly in prepared pan. Sprinkle peanut brittle crunch topping and chocolate morsels over batter in pan.

Bake 30 minutes. Cool in pan on wire rack 10 minutes. Cut into sixteen 2-inch squares and remove from pan.

16 squares

Quick PRUNE-IN-THE-MIDDLE BARS

2½ cups all-purpose flour
¾ cup sugar, divided
1 tablespoon baking powder
½ teaspoon salt
⅔ cup butter or margarine, softened
1 egg, beaten
⅓ cup milk

1 can Solo or 1 jar Baker Prune Filling
1 teaspoon cinnamon
1 teaspoon grated lemon peel
Milk for brushing
Sugar for sprinkling

Preheat oven to 375°F.

Stir flour, ¼ cup sugar, baking powder, and salt in medium-size bowl until blended. Cut in butter until mixture resembles coarse crumbs. Add egg and milk and mix until dough binds together. Knead in bowl 5 to 7 strokes or until smooth.

Divide dough in half. Roll out 1 piece of dough to 14 x 10-inch rectangle. Fit dough into bottom and up sides of ungreased 13 x 9-inch baking pan.

Spread prune filling over dough. Stir remaining ½ cup sugar, cinnamon, and lemon peel in small bowl. Sprinkle over prune filling.

Roll out remaining piece of dough to 13 x 9-inch rectangle and place over filling. Brush top lightly with milk and sprinkle with sugar.

Bake 25 to 30 minutes or until top is golden brown. Cool completely in pan on wire rack. Cut into eighteen 2⅛ x 3-inch bars.

18 bars

Easy APRICOT OATMEAL BARS

1½ cups all-purpose flour
¾ cup firmly packed brown sugar
1 teaspoon baking powder
1 cup butter or margarine, softened
1½ cups quick-cooking rolled oats

½ cup flaked coconut
½ cup coarsely chopped walnuts
1 can Solo or 1 jar Baker Apricot, Raspberry, or Strawberry Filling

Preheat oven to 350°F. Grease 13 x 9-inch baking pan and set aside.

Combine flour, brown sugar, and baking powder in medium-size bowl. Cut in butter until mixture resembles coarse crumbs. Add oats, coconut, and walnuts, and mix until crumbly. Press half of mixture into prepared pan.

Spoon apricot filling over crumb mixture in pan. Sprinkle remaining crumb mixture over apricot layer.

Bake 25 to 30 minutes or until lightly browned. (Center may seem soft but will set when cool.) Cool completely in pan on wire rack. Cut into thirty-six 1½ x 2⅛-inch bars.

36 bars

RASPBERRY MERINGUE BARS

1 cup butter or margarine, softened	2 cups all-purpose flour
½ cup firmly packed brown sugar	1 can Solo or 1 jar Baker Raspberry
1 egg	Filling

Meringue Topping:

3 egg whites	½ cup flaked or shredded coconut
¾ cup granulated sugar	½ cup slivered almonds

Preheat oven to 325°F. Grease 13 x 9-inch baking pan and set aside.

Beat butter and brown sugar in medium-size bowl with electric mixer until light and fluffy. Add egg and beat until blended. Stir in flour until well combined. Pat dough evenly in prepared pan.

Bake 20 minutes. Remove from oven and spread raspberry filling over crust. (Do not turn oven off.)

To make meringue topping, beat egg whites in medium-size bowl with electric mixer until soft peaks form. Add granulated sugar gradually and beat until stiff and glossy. Fold coconut and slivered almonds into beaten egg whites. Spread over raspberry filling. Return to oven and bake 20 minutes or until meringue topping is lightly browned. Cool completely in pan on wire rack. Cut into forty-eight 1½ x 1⅝-inch bars.

48 bars

NEAPOLITAN COOKIES

1½ cups butter or margarine, softened	4 to 6 drops red food coloring
1 cup sugar	1 can Solo or 1 jar Baker Raspberry
1 can Solo Almond Paste	Filling
4 eggs	4 squares (4 ounces) semisweet
1 teaspoon almond extract	chocolate, coarsely chopped
2 cups all-purpose flour	2 teaspoons vegetable shortening
4 to 6 drops green food coloring	

Preheat oven to 350°F. Grease 13 x 9-inch baking pan, line with waxed paper, and grease paper. Line large baking sheet with aluminum foil and set aside.

Beat butter and sugar in large bowl with electric mixer until light and fluffy. Break almond paste into small pieces and add about one-third at a time, beating well after each addition, until mixture is smooth. Add eggs and almond extract and beat until well combined. Beat in flour until thoroughly blended.

Divide batter into thirds. Place one-third in bowl, add green food coloring, mix until evenly blended, and set aside. Place second third in separate bowl, add red food coloring, mix until evenly blended, and set aside. Spread remaining plain batter in lined baking pan.

Bake 20 minutes or until top is lightly browned. Cool in pan on wire rack 5 minutes. Invert onto rack, remove pan, and carefully peel off lining paper.

Reline pan and repeat with pink batter. Reline pan and repeat with green batter.

Place green layer on foil-lined baking sheet and spread with half of raspberry filling. Top with plain layer and spread with remaining raspberry filling. Top with pink layer and press down gently. Wrap tightly with aluminum foil and refrigerate overnight.

Place chocolate and shortening in small saucepan and cook over low heat, stirring, until melted and smooth. Let cool slightly. Unwrap layers and trim off any crusty edges. Spread chocolate over top of pink layer. Let stand until chocolate is dry and set. Cut into squares about 1 inch in size.

About 108 cookies

1: *Spread half the raspberry filling over one layer and top with second layer.*

2: *Use both hands to place top cake layer over filling.*

3: *Spread melted chocolate over top layer and let stand until chocolate is set.*

CHOCOLATE-DIPPED ALMOND HORNS

1 can Solo Almond Paste
3 egg whites
½ cup superfine sugar
½ teaspoon almond extract

¼ cup plus 2 tablespoons all-purpose flour
½ cup sliced almonds
5 squares (5 ounces) semisweet chocolate, melted and cooled

Preheat oven to 350°F. Grease 2 baking sheets and set aside.

Break almond paste into small pieces and place in medium-size bowl or container of food processor. Add egg whites, sugar, and almond extract, and beat with electric mixer or process until mixture is very smooth. Add flour and beat or process until blended.

Spoon almond mixture into pastry bag fitted with ½-inch (#8) plain tip. Pipe mixture into 5- or 6-inch crescents on prepared baking sheets about 1½ inches apart. Sprinkle with sliced almonds.

Bake 13 to 15 minutes or until edges are golden. Cool on baking sheets on wire racks 2 minutes. Remove from baking sheets and cool completely on racks. Dip ends of cookies in melted chocolate and place on sheet of aluminum foil. Let stand until chocolate is set.

About 16 cookies   *(see photo page 70)*

ICE CREAM KOLACKY

4 cups all-purpose flour
2 cups butter or margarine
1 pint vanilla ice cream, slightly softened

2 cans Solo or 2 jars Baker Filling (any flavor)

Sift flour into large bowl. Cut in butter until mixture resembles coarse crumbs. Cut ice cream into small chunks and add to flour mixture. Cut in with pastry blender until ice cream absorbs flour and dough binds together. Knead dough in bowl 5 to 8 strokes or until smooth. Divide dough into 3 equal-size pieces. Wrap each piece in plastic wrap and refrigerate 1 hour.

Preheat oven to 400°F.

Roll out 1 piece of dough on lightly floured surface to ¼-inch thickness. Cut with floured 2½-inch plain or fluted cookie cutter. Place cookies on ungreased baking sheets about 1 inch apart. Spoon level teaspoonful of filling onto center of each cookie. Repeat with remaining dough and filling.

Bake 12 to 15 minutes or until cookies are golden. Remove from baking sheets and cool completely on wire racks.

About 84 cookies

ALMOND RASPBERRY THUMBPRINT COOKIES

1 cup butter or margarine, softened
1 cup sugar
1 can Solo or 1 jar Baker Almond
    Filling
2 egg yolks
1 teaspoon almond extract

2½ cups all-purpose flour
½ teaspoon baking powder
½ teaspoon salt
1 can Solo or 1 jar Baker Raspberry
    or Strawberry Filling

Beat butter and sugar in medium-size bowl with electric mixer until light and fluffy. Add almond filling, egg yolks, and almond extract, and beat until blended. Stir in flour, baking powder, and salt with wooden spoon to make soft dough. Cover bowl and refrigerate at least 3 hours or overnight.

Preheat oven to 350°F.

Shape dough into 1-inch walnut-size balls. Place on ungreased baking sheets about 1½ inches apart. Press thumb into center of each ball to make deep depression. Spoon ½ teaspoon raspberry filling into depressions.

Bake 11 to 13 minutes or until edges of cookies are golden brown. Cool on baking sheets on wire racks 1 minute. Remove from baking sheets and cool completely on racks.

About 60 cookies

Easy   NUT RUM BALLS

1 package (12 ounces) vanilla wafers
About 2 cups confectioners
    sugar
2 tablespoons unsweetened cocoa
    powder

1 can Solo or 1 jar Baker Nut Filling
¼ cup dark rum or brandy
3 tablespoons dark corn syrup

Line 2 baking sheets with waxed paper and set aside.

Place vanilla wafers in heavy-duty plastic bag and crush with rolling pin to make fine crumbs, or place wafers in food processor and process until fine. You should have about 3 cups crumbs.

Place wafer crumbs in large bowl. Add 1 cup confectioners sugar and cocoa powder. Stir until blended. Add nut filling, rum, and corn syrup, and mix until well combined.

Dust hands generously with confectioners sugar. Shape mixture into 1-inch balls. Roll balls in confectioners sugar and place on lined baking sheets. Let stand several hours or overnight before serving to allow flavors to blend. Store in airtight containers.

About 45 cookies

RUGELACH

¾ cup butter or margarine, softened
1 cup sugar
3 eggs
2 tablespoons maple syrup

3¾ cups all-purpose flour
2 teaspoons baking powder
1 teaspoon cinnamon
½ teaspoon salt

Filling:
1 can Solo or 1 jar Baker Nut Filling
1 cup finely chopped nuts (walnuts, almonds, hazelnuts, or pecans)
½ cup currants
½ cup milk

1 teaspoon brandy extract or rum extract
6 tablespoons melted butter or margarine for brushing
Sugar for sprinkling (optional)

Beat butter, sugar, eggs, and maple syrup in large bowl with electric mixer until thoroughly blended. Combine flour, baking powder, cinnamon, and salt. Add to butter mixture gradually, beating constantly to make stiff, pliable dough. Divide dough into 3 equal-size pieces, wrap each piece separately in waxed paper, and refrigerate 3 to 4 hours or overnight.

To make filling, combine nut filling, chopped nuts, currants, milk, and brandy extract in medium-size bowl. Stir until blended and set aside.

1: *Spread filling over dough. Cut dough in half.*

2: *Cut each half of dough into eleven 1-inch-wide strips. Roll up each strip jelly-roll style.*

3: *Place filled spirals seamside down on lined baking sheets.*

Preheat oven to 350°F. Grease baking sheets and line with parchment paper or aluminum foil.

Roll out 1 piece of dough on lightly floured surface with floured rolling pin. Roll to 11-inch square and brush with melted butter. Spread one-third of nut filling evenly over dough. Cut dough in half lengthwise. Cut each half into eleven 1-inch-wide strips with pizza cutter or sharp knife. Roll strips, jelly-roll style, and place, seam side down, on lined baking sheets about 1 inch apart. Brush with melted butter and sprinkle with sugar, if desired. Repeat with remaining dough and filling.

Bake 18 to 20 minutes or until golden brown. Cool on baking sheets on wire racks 1 minute. Remove from baking sheets and cool completely on racks.

About 66 cookies

FILLED CHEESE DREAMS

2 packages (8 ounces each) cream cheese, softened
1 cup butter, softened
½ cup firmly packed brown sugar
About 2 cups all-purpose flour

1 can Solo or 1 jar Baker Fruit Filling (any flavor)
1 egg yolk beaten with 1 tablespoon milk for brushing

Beat cream cheese, butter, and brown sugar in large bowl with electric mixer until light and fluffy. Stir in enough flour to make stiff dough. Divide dough in half. Wrap each piece separately in plastic wrap and refrigerate 30 minutes.

Preheat oven to 350°F.

Remove 1 piece of dough from refrigerator and divide into 36 equal-size balls. Press balls into bottom and halfway up side of ungreased 1¾-inch miniature muffin pans. Spoon about ½ teaspoon filling into each lined muffin cup.

Divide remaining piece of dough into 36 equal-size balls. Flatten balls and place over filling. Lightly press edges to seal. Prick tops lightly with fork to make vent. Brush tops with beaten egg yolk mixture.

Bake 25 to 30 minutes or until tops are golden brown. Cool in pans on wire racks 10 minutes. Remove from pans and cool completely on racks.

36 pastries

HAMANTASCHEN

2¾ cups all-purpose flour
½ cup sugar
1 tablespoon baking powder
1 teaspoon grated orange peel
½ teaspoon salt
1 cup butter or margarine, softened

2 eggs, beaten
2 tablespoons milk
1 can Solo or 1 jar Baker Poppy or
    Prune Filling
1 egg yolk beaten with 1 tablespoon
    milk for brushing

Stir flour, sugar, baking powder, orange peel, and salt in large bowl. Cut in butter until mixture resembles coarse crumbs. Add eggs and milk and mix until dough binds together. Knead dough in bowl 5 to 8 strokes or until smooth. Divide dough in half and wrap each piece separately in waxed paper or plastic wrap. Refrigerate 1 hour.

Preheat oven to 350°F. Grease 2 baking sheets and set aside.

Roll out 1 piece of dough on lightly floured surface to ¼-inch thickness. Cut dough with floured 3-inch round plain cookie cutter. Spoon 1 teaspoonful poppy filling onto center of each circle. Bring 3 edges of circle together into middle of circle to form triangle. Pinch edges upward to make slight ridge, leaving small hole in center. Place on prepared baking sheets about 1½ inches apart and brush with beaten egg yolk mixture. Repeat with remaining dough and filling.

Bake 20 to 25 minutes or until golden brown. Remove from baking sheets and cool completely on wire racks.

About 32 cookies

1: *Spoon poppy filling onto the cut circles of dough.*

2: *Bring 3 edges of dough together into middle of circle.*

3: *Pinch edges upward to make slight ridge.*

EUROPEAN KOLACKY

1 cup butter or margarine, softened
1 package (8 ounces) cream cheese,
   softened
1 tablespoon milk
1 tablespoon sugar
1 egg yolk

1½ cups all-purpose flour
½ teaspoon baking powder
1 can Solo or 1 jar Baker Filling
   (any flavor)
Confectioners sugar

Beat butter, cream cheese, milk, and sugar in medium-size bowl with electric mixer until thoroughly blended. Beat in egg yolk. Sift flour and baking powder and stir into butter mixture to make stiff dough. Cover bowl and refrigerate several hours or overnight.

Preheat oven to 400°F.

Roll out dough on lightly floured surface to ¼-inch thickness. Cut dough with floured 2-inch cookie cutter. Place cookies on ungreased baking sheets about 1 inch apart. Make depression in center of cookies with thumb or back of spoon. Spoon 1 teaspoon filling into center of cookies.

Bake 10 to 12 minutes or until lightly browned. Remove from baking sheets and cool completely on wire racks. Sprinkle with confectioners sugar just before serving.

About 36 cookies

PEANUT BUTTER COOKIES

⅔ cup butter or margarine, softened
½ cup chunky peanut butter
½ cup granulated sugar
¾ cup firmly packed brown sugar
2 eggs
1 teaspoon vanilla

2¼ cups all-purpose flour
1 teaspoon baking soda
½ teaspoon salt
1 egg white, lightly beaten
1 can Solo Peanut Brittle Crunch
Topping

Place butter, peanut butter, and sugars in medium-size bowl and beat with electric mixer until light and fluffy. Add eggs and vanilla and beat until blended. Stir in flour, baking soda, and salt with wooden spoon to make stiff dough. Cover bowl and refrigerate 2 hours.

Preheat oven to 350°F. Grease 2 baking sheets and set aside.

Shape dough into 1-inch walnut-size balls. Dip balls into beaten egg white and then roll in peanut brittle crunch topping. Place balls on prepared baking sheets 2 inches apart. Flatten balls slightly with bottom of juice glass.

Bake 8 to 10 minutes or until edges of cookies are golden brown. Remove from baking sheets and cool completely on wire racks.

About 60 cookies

TEATIME TREATS

2 packages (3 ounces each) cream
cheese, softened
1 cup butter or margarine, softened

2 tablespoons sugar
2 cups all-purpose flour

Filling:

½ cup sugar
2 eggs
¼ cup all-purpose flour
1 teaspoon vanilla

1 can Solo or 1 jar Baker Apricot
Filling
½ cup chopped nuts (optional)

Preheat oven to 350°F.

Beat cream cheese, butter, and sugar in medium-size bowl with electric mixer until fluffy. Stir in flour to make soft dough. Divide dough in half. Shape each piece of dough into about twenty-four 1-inch balls. Press balls into bottom and up side of ungreased 1¾-inch miniature muffin pans. Set aside.

To make filling, beat sugar, eggs, flour, vanilla, and apricot filling in medium-size bowl with electric mixer until blended. Stir in nuts. Spoon evenly into pastry-lined muffin cups.

Bake 25 to 30 minutes or until filling is set and crust is golden. Cool completely in pans on wire racks.

About 48 cookies   *(see photo pages 52-53)*

Quick
CHOCOLATE PEANUT BRITTLE NO-BAKE COOKIES

1 cup granulated sugar
1 cup firmly packed brown sugar
½ cup milk
½ cup butter or margarine
¾ cup peanut butter

2 squares (2 ounces) semisweet
   chocolate, chopped
2 cups quick-cooking rolled oats
½ cup Solo Peanut Brittle Crunch
   Topping
½ cup flaked or shredded coconut

Line baking sheets with waxed paper and set aside.

Place sugars, milk, and butter in large saucepan. Cook over medium heat, stirring constantly, until butter is melted and mixture comes to a boil. Boil 1 minute.

Remove from heat. Add peanut butter and chocolate and stir until chocolate is melted and mixture is smooth. Add oats, peanut brittle crunch topping, and coconut, and stir until well mixed. Drop mixture by rounded teaspoonfuls onto lined baking sheets. Let stand until completely cool and set. Peel cookies off lining paper. Store in cool place.

About 48 cookies   *(see photo pages 52-53)*

APRICOT PINWHEEL SLICES

2 cups sifted all-purpose flour
1 cup butter or margarine, softened
1 cup dairy sour cream
1 can Solo or 1 jar Baker Apricot,
   Raspberry, or Strawberry Filling

1 cup flaked coconut
1 cup finely chopped pecans
Confectioners sugar

Place flour in medium-size bowl. Cut in butter until mixture resembles coarse crumbs. Add sour cream and stir until blended. Divide dough into 4 equal-size pieces. Wrap each piece separately in plastic wrap or waxed paper and refrigerate 2 to 4 hours.

Preheat oven to 350°F.

Roll out dough, 1 piece at a time, on lightly floured surface to 6 x 12-inch rectangle. Spread one-fourth of apricot filling over dough and sprinkle with ¼ cup coconut and ¼ cup pecans. Roll up, jelly-roll style, starting from short side. Pinch seam to seal. Place, seam side down, on ungreased baking sheet. Repeat with remaining dough, apricot filling, coconut, and pecans.

Bake 40 to 45 minutes or until rolls are golden brown. Remove from baking sheets and place on wire racks. Dust liberally with confectioners sugar while still warm. Cool completely on racks. Cut into 1-inch slices.

About 24 cookies

SUGAR CRUNCH COOKIES

1 cup butter or margarine, softened
1 package (3 ounces) cream cheese, softened
1 cup sugar
1 egg
1 teaspoon vanilla

1 can Solo Crunch Topping (any kind)
2⅓ cups all-purpose flour
½ teaspoon baking soda
Sugar for sprinkling

Beat butter, cream cheese, and sugar in medium-size bowl with electric mixer until light and fluffy. Add egg and vanilla and beat until blended. Stir in crunch topping. Stir in flour and baking soda to make soft dough. Cover bowl and refrigerate 2 to 3 hours.

Preheat oven to 350°F.

Shape dough into balls about 1 inch in diameter. Place balls on ungreased baking sheets about 2 inches apart. Dip prongs of fork into flour and press across top of cookies to flatten. Press again in opposite direction. Sprinkle cookies with sugar.

Bake 11 minutes or just until golden. Remove from baking sheets and cool completely on wire racks.

About 48 cookies

Easy   PRUNE BARS

2 cups all-purpose flour
1 cup sugar
1 teaspoon salt
½ teaspoon baking soda
¾ cup butter or margarine, softened

1½ cups shredded or flaked coconut
1 cup chopped nuts (walnuts, pecans, or almonds)
1 can Solo or 1 jar Baker Prune or Date Filling

Preheat oven to 400°F. Grease 13 x 9-inch baking pan and set aside.

Combine flour, sugar, salt, and baking soda in medium-size bowl and stir until blended. Cut in butter until mixture resembles coarse crumbs. Add coconut and chopped nuts and stir until well mixed. Measure 2 cups flour coconut mixture and set aside. Press remaining mixture into bottom of prepared pan.

Bake 10 minutes. Remove from oven and spread prune filling over baked crust. Sprinkle reserved flour coconut mixture over prune filling. Bake 15 minutes or until top is golden brown. Cool completely in pan on wire rack. Cut into thirty-six 1½ x 2⅛-inch bars.

36 bars

Chocolate-Dipped Almond Horns (page 62), Sugar Crunch Cookies, Prune Bars (opposite)

Easy   ALMOND MACAROONS

1 can Solo Almond Paste   1¼ cups sugar
2 egg whites

Preheat oven to 325°F. Line baking sheets with parchment paper or brown paper.

Break almond paste into small pieces and place in medium-size bowl or container of food processor. Add egg whites and sugar and beat with electric mixer or process until mixture is very smooth.

Spoon almond mixture into large pastry bag fitted with open star tip. Pipe into stars or drop by rounded teaspoonfuls onto lined baking sheets about 1 inch apart.

Bake 20 minutes or until lightly browned. Cool completely on baking sheets on wire racks. Peel macaroons off parchment paper when completely cool. Store in airtight containers.

About 36 cookies

Note: To remove macaroons from brown paper, brush underside of paper with water under each cookie, 1 at a time.

ALMOND CRESCENTS

1 cup butter or margarine, softened   1 can Solo or 1 jar Baker Almond
⅓ cup sugar   Filling
1 teaspoon almond extract   2 cups all-purpose flour
                                                              Confectioners sugar

Beat butter and sugar in large bowl with electric mixer until light and fluffy. Beat in almond extract and almond filling until blended. Stir in flour with wooden spoon to make stiff dough. Cover and refrigerate at least 4 hours or until dough is no longer sticky.

Preheat oven to 325°F.

Dust hands with flour. Shape teaspoonfuls of dough into small tapered crescents about 2½ inches long. Place on ungreased baking sheets about 1½ inches apart.

Bake 15 to 20 minutes or until cookies are firm and lightly browned. Cool on baking sheets on wire racks 1 minute. Remove from baking sheets and cool on racks. Dust with confectioners sugar while cookies are still warm. Cool completely. Store in airtight containers.

About 48 cookies

Easy   ALMOND CHINESE CHEWS

1 cup sugar
3 eggs
1 can Solo or 1 jar Baker Almond
    Filling

¾ cup all-purpose flour
1 teaspoon baking powder
¼ teaspoon salt
    Confectioners sugar

Preheat oven to 300°F. Grease 13 x 9-inch baking pan and set aside.

Beat sugar and eggs in medium-size bowl with electric mixer until thoroughly blended. Add almond filling and beat until blended. Stir flour, baking powder, and salt until mixed, and fold into almond mixture. Spread batter evenly in prepared pan.

Bake 40 to 45 minutes or until toothpick inserted in center comes out clean. Cool completely in pan on wire rack. Cut into thirty-six 1½ x 2⅛-inch bars and dust with confectioners sugar.

36 bars

CHAPTER 5

Pies, Pastries, and Cheesecakes

Poppy Cream Cheesecake (page 93), Fresh Strawberry Pie (page 76)

Quick FRESH STRAWBERRY PIE

1 quart (2 pints) strawberries
1 jar Solo Strawberry Glaze
1 baked 9-inch pie shell

Sweetened whipped cream to serve
(optional)

Wash and hull strawberries and pat dry. Place berries in medium-size bowl, add glaze, and toss gently to coat. Arrange in baked pie shell. Refrigerate until thoroughly chilled. Serve with whipped cream, if desired.

6 to 8 servings   *(see photo pages 74-75)*

Variation: Substitute 2 pints blueberries or 6 to 8 medium-size peaches, peeled and sliced, for strawberries. Substitute blueberry or peach glaze for strawberry glaze.

WHITE CHOCOLATE MOUSSE PIE

Chocolate Wafer Crumb Crust:

1¼ cups chocolate wafer crumbs
    (about 32 chocolate wafers)
¼ cup ground pecans

5 tablespoons butter or
    margarine, melted

Filling:

9 ounces white chocolate,
    coarsely chopped
⅓ cup milk
1 cup heavy cream
1 tablespoon white crème de cacao
2 egg whites

1 can Solo or 1 jar Baker
    Raspberry Filling
Grated white or dark chocolate,
    or chocolate leaves or curls
    to decorate

Preheat oven to 350°F. Grease 9-inch pie plate and set aside.

To make crust, combine chocolate wafer crumbs and ground pecans in bowl. Add melted butter and stir until well blended. Press crumb mixture in bottom and up side of prepared pie plate. Bake 8 to 10 minutes. Cool completely on wire rack.

To make filling, place chocolate and milk in top of double boiler set over (not in) pan of barely simmering water. Cook, stirring constantly, until chocolate is melted and mixture is smooth. Pour chocolate into large bowl and set aside to cool to room temperature.

Whip cream with electric mixer until soft peaks form. Add crème de cacao and whip until firm. Spoon 2 to 3 tablespoons whipped cream over cooled chocolate and stir well to lighten chocolate. Fold in remaining whipped cream.

Beat egg whites in clean bowl with electric mixer until stiff peaks form. Fold beaten egg whites into chocolate mixture.

Spread three-fourths of raspberry filling over cooled crust. Spoon chocolate mousse over filling. Refrigerate 30 minutes.

Spoon remaining raspberry filling around edge of pie. Decorate top of pie with grated chocolate or chocolate leaves or curls. Freeze 2 hours or overnight.

8 to 10 servings

PUMPKIN DATE CHIFFON PIE

3 eggs
1 envelope plus 1 teaspoon
   unflavored gelatin
¼ cup cold water
1 can (16 ounces) solid-pack pumpkin
½ cup firmly packed brown sugar
½ cup evaporated milk
½ cup coarsely chopped pecans

1 teaspoon pumpkin pie spice
½ cup granulated sugar
1 can Solo or 1 jar Baker Date Filling
1 baked 9-inch pie shell
½ cup heavy cream
1 tablespoon confectioners sugar
½ teaspoon vanilla

Separate eggs and set egg whites aside to come to room temperature. Sprinkle gelatin over water in small bowl and set aside.

Combine egg yolks, pumpkin, brown sugar, and milk in medium-size saucepan. Cook over medium heat, stirring constantly, until mixture is hot. Remove from heat. Add gelatin and stir until dissolved. Add pecans and pumpkin pie spice, and stir until blended. Pour into large bowl. Cover and refrigerate about 30 minutes or until mixture begins to set.

Beat egg whites in medium-size bowl with electric mixer until soft peaks form. Add granulated sugar gradually and beat until stiff and glossy. Fold into pumpkin mixture.

Spread date filling evenly over bottom of baked pie shell. Pour pumpkin mixture over filling. Refrigerate 2 to 3 hours or until set.

Whip cream in medium-size bowl with electric mixer until soft peaks form. Add confectioners sugar and vanilla and whip until firm. Spread over chilled pie or top individual servings with dollops of whipped cream.

8 servings

QUICK MANDARIN PIE

1 package (8 ounces) cream
   cheese, softened
1 package (3 ounces) cream
   cheese, softened
¼ cup sugar
1 teaspoon vanilla

1 baked 9-inch graham cracker crust
   (page 88) or 9-inch chocolate
   wafer crumb crust (page 76)*
1 cup Solo Fruit Salad Dressing
1 can (11 ounces) mandarin
   oranges, drained
Fresh mint sprig to
   decorate (optional)

Beat cream cheese, sugar, and vanilla in medium-size bowl with electric mixer until light and fluffy. Pour into crust and smooth top. Refrigerate 1 hour or until firm.

Spread fruit salad dressing evenly over cream cheese. Arrange mandarin oranges in decorative pattern on top. Refrigerate until ready to serve. Decorate with mint sprig just before serving, if desired.

6 servings

*Note: You can substitute 1 ready-made 9-inch graham cracker crust or 1 ready-made 6-ounce chocolate-flavored crumb crust.

Easy   PECAN CUSTARD PIE

1 can Solo Pecan Filling
2 eggs
½ cup sugar
1 teaspoon vanilla
⅓ cup butter or margarine, melted
½ cup dark corn syrup

2 tablespoons bourbon or dark
  rum (optional)
1 unbaked 9-inch pie shell
¾ cup pecan halves
Sweetened whipped cream to serve

Preheat oven to 375°F.

Beat pecan filling, eggs, sugar, and vanilla in medium-size bowl with electric mixer until well mixed. Add melted butter, corn syrup, and bourbon, and beat just until blended. Pour into unbaked pie shell. Arrange pecan halves in concentric circles on top of filling.

Bake 30 to 35 minutes or until tip of knife inserted in center comes out clean. Cool on wire rack. Serve warm with sweetened whipped cream.

6 to 8 servings

ALMOND CRUNCH CHOCOLATE CHIFFON PIE

2 eggs, separated
1 cup milk
½ cup granulated sugar
1 envelope unflavored gelatin
4 squares (4 ounces) semisweet
  chocolate, coarsely chopped
3 tablespoons amaretto liqueur

1 cup heavy cream
2 tablespoons confectioners sugar
1 cup Solo Toasted Almond Crunch
  Topping, divided
1 baked 9-inch pie shell or 9-inch
  chocolate wafer crumb crust
  (page 76)

Place egg yolks, milk, and granulated sugar in medium-size saucepan and beat with wire whisk until blended. Sprinkle gelatin over mixture and beat until blended. Stir in chocolate. Place saucepan over low heat and cook, stirring constantly, until chocolate is melted and gelatin is dissolved. Remove from heat and pour mixture into large bowl. Stir in liqueur and beat at high speed with electric mixer 2 minutes or until mixture is thick and syrupy. Refrigerate 45 minutes or until mixture mounds when dropped from spoon. Remove from refrigerator and beat 2 minutes or until fluffy.

Whip cream in separate bowl with electric mixer until soft peaks form. Add confectioners sugar and whip until firm. Set aside 1 cup whipped cream. Fold remaining 1 cup whipped cream into chocolate mixture. Fold in ¾ cup toasted almond crunch topping. Beat egg whites in separate bowl with electric mixer until stiff peaks form. Fold into chocolate-crunch mixture. Pour mixture into baked pie shell and smooth top. Refrigerate 3 to 4 hours.

When ready to serve, decorate top of pie with reserved 1 cup whipped cream and sprinkle with remaining ¼ cup toasted almond crunch topping.

6 to 8 servings

CHERRY ENVELOPES

2 packages (3 ounces each) cream
    cheese, softened
⅓ cup butter or margarine, softened
⅓ cup sugar
⅓ cup milk
2¼ cups all-purpose flour
1 teaspoon baking powder

1 teaspoon grated lemon peel
½ teaspoon salt
1 can Solo or 1 jar Baker Cherry or
    Blueberry Filling
1 egg beaten with 1 tablespoon water
    for brushing
Confectioners sugar

Preheat oven to 350°F. Grease 2 baking sheets and set aside.

Beat cream cheese, butter, sugar, and milk in large bowl with electric mixer until well blended. Stir in flour, baking powder, lemon peel, and salt. Knead dough in bowl 8 to 10 strokes or until smooth. Divide dough into 2 equal-size pieces.

Roll out 1 piece of dough on lightly floured surface to 10 x 15-inch rectangle. Cut into six 5-inch squares.

Spoon 1 heaping tablespoonful cherry filling onto center of each pastry square. Brush edges of pastry with beaten egg mixture and bring corners in to center to enclose filling. Pinch edges to seal. Place filled pastries on prepared baking sheets and brush with beaten egg mixture. Repeat with remaining pastry and cherry filling.

Bake 20 to 25 minutes or until golden brown. Remove from baking sheets and cool on wire racks. Dust with confectioners sugar just before serving.

12 pastries

Bring corners in to center to enclose filling. Pinch edges to seal.

BLUEBERRY CURAÇAO PIE

1 envelope unflavored gelatin
¼ cup cold water
2 cans Solo or 2 jars Baker
    Blueberry Filling
2 tablespoons lemon juice
1 teaspoon grated lemon peel
⅓ cup granulated sugar
¼ cup Curaçao liqueur or
    orange juice

1 package (3 ounces) cream
    cheese, softened
½ cup sifted confectioners sugar
½ cup dairy sour cream
1 cup heavy cream
1 baked 9-inch pie shell or 9-inch
    graham cracker crust (page 88)
Sweetened whipped cream
    to decorate (optional)

Sprinkle gelatin over water in small bowl and let stand 5 to 10 minutes to soften.

Place blueberry filling, lemon juice, lemon peel, and granulated sugar in medium-size saucepan and stir well. Stir in gelatin. Place over medium heat and cook, stirring, until sugar and gelatin are dissolved and mixture comes just to boiling point. Remove from heat and pour into large bowl. Set aside to cool 10 minutes. Stir in Curaçao and let cool to room temperature. Cover and refrigerate until mixture mounds when dropped from spoon, about 25 minutes.

Whip cream cheese and confectioners sugar in medium-size bowl with electric mixer until blended and smooth. Add sour cream and beat just until blended.

Whip cream in separate bowl until firm. Fold whipped cream into cream cheese mixture. Fold cream cheese mixture into blueberry mixture. Spoon into baked pie shell and smooth top. Refrigerate several hours or until set. Decorate with sweetened whipped cream just before serving, if desired.

8 servings

Quick # FROZEN STRAWBERRY PIE

1 quart vanilla ice cream, softened
1 can Solo or 1 jar Baker Strawberry,
    Raspberry, Cherry, or
    Blueberry Filling

1 baked 9-inch pie shell or 9-inch
    chocolate wafer crumb crust
    (page 76)
1 cup hot fudge topping

Spoon ice cream into large bowl. Add strawberry filling and stir until blended. Pour into baked pie shell and smooth top. Cover with plastic wrap and freeze until firm.

Remove pie from freezer and place in refrigerator 15 to 20 minutes before serving to soften.

Heat fudge topping until warm. Cut pie into serving pieces and spoon warmed fudge topping over each serving. Serve immediately.

8 servings

Variations: Omit hot fudge topping. Grate 3 squares (3 ounces) semisweet chocolate and sprinkle over top of pie, sprinkle any Solo Crunch Topping over pie, or spread pineapple or strawberry topping over pie.

Easy FROZEN APRICOT PARFAIT PIE

1 can Solo or 1 jar Baker Apricot,
  Strawberry, Raspberry, or
  Pineapple Filling
⅔ cup sugar
½ cup water
2 egg whites
1½ teaspoons vanilla

1 teaspoon lemon juice
1 cup heavy cream
1 baked 9-inch pie shell or 9-inch
  graham cracker crust (page 88)
Grated chocolate or chocolate curls
  to decorate

Place apricot filling in large bowl and set aside. Beat sugar, water, egg whites, vanilla, and lemon juice in medium-size bowl at low speed with electric mixer until foamy. Increase speed to high and beat 5 minutes or until soft peaks form. Stir one-third of beaten egg whites into apricot filling to lighten. Fold in remaining egg whites.

Whip cream in separate bowl until firm. Fold whipped cream into apricot mixture. Pour into baked pie shell, mounding mixture in center.

Freeze 4 to 5 hours or until firm. Transfer pie to refrigerator 10 to 15 minutes before serving to soften slightly. Decorate with grated chocolate or chocolate curls.

8 servings

Easy COFFEE APRICOT PIE

1 package (8 ounces) cream
  cheese, softened
1 container (8 ounces) coffee yogurt
2 to 3 tablespoons strong black coffee
¼ cup sugar or to taste
1 teaspoon vanilla
¾ cup heavy cream, whipped, or
  1½ cups frozen non-dairy
  whipped topping, thawed

1 baked 9-inch graham cracker crust
  (page 88) or 9-inch chocolate
  wafer crumb crust (page 76)*
1 can Solo or 1 jar Baker
  Apricot Filling
⅓ cup toasted sliced almonds

Beat cream cheese in medium-size bowl with electric mixer until fluffy. Add yogurt and beat just until blended. Add coffee, sugar, and vanilla, and beat until well combined. Fold in whipped cream. Pour half of cream cheese mixture into bottom of crumb crust and refrigerate 1 hour. Set remaining cream cheese mixture aside.

Spoon apricot filling over top of pie and cover with reserved cream cheese mixture. Freeze pie 2 hours.

Sprinkle almonds on pie and press down gently. Return to freezer and freeze until firm.

Transfer pie to refrigerator to soften 20 minutes before serving.

6 to 8 servings

*Note: You can substitute 1 ready-made 9-inch graham cracker crust or 1 ready-made 6-ounce chocolate-flavored crumb crust.

MOHN (POPPY) STRUDEL

1 can Solo or 1 jar Baker
Poppy Filling
⅓ cup raisins, finely chopped
1 teaspoon grated lemon peel
3 tablespoons lemon juice

1 package (16 ounces) phyllo dough
About 1 cup unsalted butter, melted
½ cup finely chopped walnuts
or pecans
Confectioners sugar

Preheat oven to 375°F. Grease large baking sheet and set aside.

Combine poppy filling, chopped raisins, lemon peel, and lemon juice in medium-size bowl and set aside.

Unfold phyllo dough and place between 2 slightly damp dish towels to keep leaves from drying out. Place 1 leaf of phyllo dough on clean dish towel and brush with melted butter. Place second leaf on top and brush with melted butter. Repeat with 8 more leaves.

Spread half of poppy filling over dough to within 1½ inches of edges all the way around. Sprinkle half of chopped nuts over filling. Fold both long sides in over filling. Fold 1 short side in about 3 inches. Continue to fold strudel over from short side, using towel as aid. Raise towel on short side and roll strudel onto prepared baking sheet, seam side down. Brush entire surface of strudel with melted butter. Repeat with remaining phyllo leaves, poppy filling, and nuts.

Bake 35 to 40 minutes or until deep golden brown. Carefully slide strudel onto wire rack to cool slightly. Dust with confectioners sugar just before serving. Serve warm.

2 strudel (16 to 20 servings)

1: *Spread filling over phyllo sheets.*   2: *Fold 1 short side of phyllo over.*

BLUEBERRY CREAM CHEESE STRUDEL

1 package (8 ounces) cream
cheese, softened
1 egg
¼ cup confectioners sugar
2 tablespoons frozen orange
juice concentrate, thawed
½ teaspoon vanilla

12 leaves (½ pound) phyllo dough
About ¾ cup unsalted butter,
melted
1 can Solo or 1 jar Baker Blueberry
Filling or any flavor Fruit Filling
Confectioners sugar

Preheat oven to 375°F. Grease large baking sheet and set aside.

Beat cream cheese, egg, and ¼ cup confectioners sugar in medium-size bowl with electric mixer until smooth. Add orange juice concentrate and vanilla and beat until blended. Set aside.

Unfold phyllo dough and place between 2 slightly damp dish towels to keep leaves from drying out. Place 1 leaf of phyllo dough on clean dish towel and brush with melted butter. Place second leaf on top and brush with melted butter. Repeat with remaining leaves.

Spread cream cheese mixture down center of dough to within 2 inches of edges on all sides. Spread blueberry filling over cream cheese mixture. Fold both long sides in over filling. Fold 1 short side in 2 inches. Continue to fold strudel over from short side, using towel as aid. Raise towel on short side and roll strudel onto prepared baking sheet, seam side down. Brush entire surface with melted butter.

Bake 35 to 45 minutes or until top is golden brown and crisp. Carefully slide strudel onto wire rack to cool slightly. Dust with confectioners sugar just before serving. Serve warm.

1 strudel (8 to 10 servings)

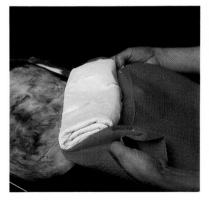

3: *Roll up phyllo with aid of towel.*   4: *Roll onto greased baking sheet.*

CHERRY SCHAUM PIE

1 recipe Vanilla Custard (page 132)
4 egg whites, room temperature
¼ teaspoon cream of tartar
¼ cup sugar
1 teaspoon vanilla
1 can Solo or 1 jar Baker
   Cherry Filling

2 to 3 tablespoons cherry-flavored
   brandy (optional)
½ cup heavy cream, whipped
½ cup coarsely chopped macadamia
   nuts, almonds, or walnuts

Prepare Vanilla Custard. Cover surface of custard with waxed paper and refrigerate until well chilled.

Preheat oven to 275°F. Grease 9- or 10-inch pie plate and set aside.

Beat egg whites and cream of tartar in large bowl with electric mixer until soft peaks form. Add sugar gradually, 2 tablespoons at a time, beating after each addition until sugar is completely dissolved. Add vanilla and beat until meringue stands in stiff, glossy peaks. Spoon into prepared pie plate and spread evenly over bottom and high up side to make shell.

Bake 1 hour. Turn oven off and let stand in oven with door closed 1 hour. Cool completely on wire rack.

Spread chilled Vanilla Custard evenly in pie shell. Place cherry filling in medium-size bowl and stir in brandy. Fold in whipped cream and spread evenly over custard. Sprinkle nuts around edge of pie. Refrigerate 1 to 2 hours before serving.

8 servings

RASPBERRY PEAR PIE

Pastry for 9-inch double-crust or lattice-topped pie:

2 cups all-purpose flour
1 teaspoon salt
6 tablespoons chilled butter

6 tablespoons chilled shortening
6 to 7 tablespoons ice water

Filling:

½ cup sugar
2 tablespoons cornstarch
½ teaspoon cinnamon
¼ teaspoon mace
4 to 5 medium-size Bartlett or Bosc
   pears, peeled, cored, and sliced

1 can Solo or 1 jar Baker Raspberry
   or Strawberry Filling
Water for brushing
Sugar for sprinkling

Stir flour and salt in medium-size bowl until blended. Cut in butter and shortening with pastry blender or 2 knives until mixture resembles coarse crumbs. Sprinkle flour mixture with ice water, 1 tablespoon at a time, and toss with fork until mixture is evenly moistened and binds together. Gather dough and shape into slightly flattened ball. Divide dough into 2 pieces, making 1 piece slightly larger than the other. Wrap each piece separately in waxed paper or plastic wrap and refrigerate 30 minutes.

Roll out 1 piece of pastry to 11-inch circle on lightly floured surface and line 9-inch pie plate. Trim pastry edge to 1 inch beyond rim of pie plate.

To make filling, combine sugar, cornstarch, cinnamon, and mace in large bowl. Add sliced pears and toss to coat. Arrange pears in pastry-lined dish and spoon raspberry filling over pears.

Preheat oven to 400°F.

Roll out remaining pastry to 11-inch circle on lightly floured surface. Cut pastry into 1-inch-wide strips. Arrange pastry strips in lattice pattern over top of pie. Fold trimmed pastry edge of lower crust over strips to build up edge. Seal and flute edge. Brush edge and lattice strips with water and sprinkle with sugar.

Bake 40 to 45 minutes or until pastry is golden brown. Cool completely on wire rack.

6 to 8 servings

Quick
PINEAPPLE APRICOT SUNDAE PIE

1 package (8 ounces) cream
   cheese, softened
1 container (8 ounces) vanilla yogurt
½ cup sugar
1 can Solo or 1 jar Baker
   Apricot Filling
1 can Solo or 1 jar Baker
   Pineapple Filling

1 container (8 ounces) frozen non-
   dairy whipped topping, thawed,
   or 1 cup heavy cream, whipped
½ cup Solo Toasted Almond
   Crunch Topping
1 baked 9-inch graham cracker crust
   (page 88) or 9-inch chocolate
   wafer crumb crust (page 76)*
6 tablespoons chocolate
   syrup, divided

Beat cream cheese in large bowl with electric mixer until fluffy. Add yogurt and sugar and beat until blended. Stir in apricot and pineapple fillings until well combined. Fold in whipped topping and toasted almond crunch topping. Pour into crumb crust and spoon 4 tablespoons chocolate syrup over top. Swirl syrup lightly through filling with flat-bladed knife. Freeze pie 3 hours.

Drizzle remaining 2 tablespoons chocolate syrup over top of pie in zig-zag pattern. Return to freezer until firm, about 2 hours. Place pie in refrigerator 20 minutes to soften before serving.

6 to 8 servings

*Note: You can substitute 1 ready-made 9-inch graham cracker crust or 1 ready-made 6-ounce chocolate-flavored crumb crust.

NO-BAKE STRAWBERRY CHEESECAKE

1 cup vanilla wafer crumbs
   (about 22 vanilla wafers)
   or graham cracker crumbs
   (about 12 graham crackers)

2 tablespoons sugar
3 tablespoons butter or margarine,
   melted and cooled

Filling:

1½ envelopes unflavored gelatin
¼ cup orange juice
⅔ cup sugar
1 can Solo or 1 jar Baker Strawberry,
   Raspberry, or Cherry Filling
1 tablespoon grated orange peel
2 tablespoons orange-flavored
   brandy (optional)

2 cups small-curd cottage
   cheese, drained
1 cup heavy cream
2 egg whites
   Sliced strawberries to
   decorate (optional)

Preheat oven to 350°F. Grease 9-inch springform pan and set aside.

Combine crumbs and sugar in small bowl. Add melted butter and stir until well blended. Press crumb mixture into bottom of prepared pan. Bake 8 to 10 minutes. Remove from oven and cool completely on wire rack.

To make filling, sprinkle gelatin over orange juice in small saucepan and let stand 5 minutes. Cook over low heat, stirring, until gelatin is dissolved. Remove from heat and pour into large bowl. Stir in sugar, strawberry filling, orange peel, and brandy. Set aside to cool.

Place cottage cheese in container of blender or food processor and process until smooth. Add to strawberry mixture and stir until blended. Refrigerate 30 minutes or until mixture mounds when dropped from spoon.

Whip cream in medium-size bowl with electric mixer until firm. Fold into strawberry mixture.

Beat egg whites in separate bowl with electric mixer until stiff peaks form. Fold into strawberry mixture. Pour mixture over cooled crust and smooth top. Refrigerate 3 to 4 hours or until set.

To serve, run tip of sharp knife around inside edge of pan and remove side of pan. Place cheesecake on serving plate and decorate top with sliced strawberries, if desired.

10 to 12 servings

No-Bake Strawberry Cheesecake (opposite), Almond Apple Tart (page 99)

Eosy FRUIT-TOPPED CHEESE PIE

Graham Cracker Crust:

1½ cups graham cracker crumbs (about 18 graham crackers)
¼ cup sugar

½ teaspoon cinnamon (optional)
5 tablespoons butter or margarine, melted and cooled

Filling:

2 packages (8 ounces each) cream cheese, softened
⅔ cup sugar
1 teaspoon vanilla
2 eggs

½ cup dairy sour cream
1 can Solo or 1 jar Baker Apricot, Pineapple, Strawberry, Blueberry, or Cherry Filling

Preheat oven to 350°F. Grease 9-inch pie plate or springform pan and set aside.

Stir cracker crumbs, sugar, and cinnamon in medium-size bowl. Add melted butter and stir until blended. Press crumb mixture onto bottom and up side of prepared pie plate. Bake 8 to 10 minutes. Cool completely on wire rack.

To make filling, beat cream cheese in medium-size bowl with electric mixer until smooth. Add sugar, vanilla, and eggs, and beat until well blended. Beat in sour cream just until mixed. Pour into prepared crust.

Bake 30 to 35 minutes or until center of pie is set. Cool completely on wire rack. Spoon apricot filling over cooled cheese pie. Refrigerate 3 to 4 hours or until ready to serve.

8 servings

Eosy INDIVIDUAL CHEESECAKES

24 vanilla wafers
2 packages (8 ounces each) cream cheese, softened
2 eggs

1 cup sugar
1 teaspoon vanilla
1 can Solo or 1 jar Baker Fruit Filling (any flavor)

Preheat oven to 375°F. Line two 12-cup muffin pans with paper cupcake liners. Place vanilla wafer in each lined muffin cup and set aside.

Place cream cheese, eggs, sugar, and vanilla in medium-size bowl or container of food processor. Beat with electric mixer or process until well blended. Spoon 1 rounded tablespoonful cheese mixture into each lined muffin cup.

Bake 20 minutes or until cheese mixture is set and tops are golden. Cool in pans on wire racks 5 minutes. Remove from pans and cool completely on racks.

Spoon 1 rounded teaspoonful fruit filling on top of each cheesecake and spread evenly with back of spoon. Refrigerate until ready to serve.

24 Individual Cheesecakes

Variation: To make miniature cheesecakes, use 72 small vanilla wafers (1⅝ inches in diameter). Bake 12 minutes in lined miniature (1⅞ x ¾-inch) muffin pans.

72 mini cheesecakes

Easy ALMOND CHEESECAKE

1 cup graham cracker crumbs
(about 12 graham crackers)
¼ cup finely ground almonds

3 tablespoons sugar
5 tablespoons butter or margarine,
melted and cooled

Topping:

1 cup dairy sour cream
2 tablespoons sugar

1 teaspoon vanilla

Filling:

2 packages (8 ounces each) cream
cheese, softened
⅓ cup sugar
3 eggs

1 can Solo or 1 jar Baker
Almond Filling
2 tablespoons all-purpose flour
1 teaspoon almond extract

Preheat oven to 350°F. Grease 9-inch springform pan and set aside.

Combine graham cracker crumbs, ground almonds, and sugar in small bowl. Add melted butter and stir until well blended. Press crumb mixture onto bottom and partly up side of prepared pan. Bake 10 minutes. Remove from oven and cool completely in pan on wire rack. (Do not turn oven off.)

To make topping, stir sour cream, sugar, and vanilla in small bowl until blended. Set aside in refrigerator.

To make filling, beat cream cheese and sugar in medium-size bowl with electric mixer until light and fluffy. Add eggs, 1 at a time, beating well after each addition. Add almond filling, flour, and almond extract, and beat until well blended. Pour into cooled crumb crust. Bake 1 hour or until center is set.

Remove cheesecake from oven and spread reserved sour cream mixture over top. Return to oven and bake 12 to 15 minutes or until topping is set. Cool completely in pan on wire rack. Refrigerate several hours or until ready to serve.

To serve, run tip of sharp knife around inside edge of pan and remove side of pan. Place cheesecake on serving plate.

12 to 14 servings

LINZER TORTE

10 tablespoons butter or
   margarine, softened
¾ cup sugar
1 egg
2 cups sifted all-purpose flour
1 teaspoon cinnamon
½ teaspoon baking powder
½ teaspoon salt

¼ teaspoon ground cloves
½ cup ground almonds
1 tablespoon milk
1 can Solo or 1 jar Baker
   Raspberry Filling
1 egg beaten with 1 tablespoon
   water for brushing
Confectioners sugar (optional)

Beat butter and sugar in large bowl with electric mixer until light and fluffy. Add egg and beat until blended. Combine flour, cinnamon, baking powder, salt, and cloves, and add to butter mixture. Stir until blended. Stir in ground almonds and milk. Shape dough into slightly flattened ball, wrap in plastic wrap or waxed paper, and refrigerate 1 hour.

Preheat oven to 350°F.

Press or pat out two-thirds of dough in bottom of ungreased 10-inch springform pan, pressing dough about ¾ inch up side of pan. Spread raspberry filling in crust.

Divide remaining dough into 10 equal-size pieces. Dust hands with flour and roll each piece into thin 10-inch rope. Arrange ropes in lattice pattern over raspberry filling, trimming ends to fit. Brush pastry with beaten egg mixture.

Bake 40 to 45 minutes or until crust is golden brown. Cool completely in pan on wire rack. Run tip of sharp knife around inside edge of pan and remove side of pan. Dust with confectioners sugar, if desired.

10 to 12 servings

Linzer Torte (opposite), Puff Pastry Apple Pockets (page 98)

Easy
RASPBERRY SWIRL CHEESECAKE

1 cup graham cracker crumbs
(about 12 graham crackers)
or chocolate wafer crumbs
(about 26 chocolate wafers)

3 tablespoons sugar
¼ cup butter, melted and cooled

Filling:

3 packages (8 ounces each) cream
cheese, softened
½ cup sugar
3 tablespoons all-purpose flour
3 eggs

1 teaspoon vanilla
1 can Solo or 1 jar Baker Raspberry,
Cherry, Blueberry, Apricot,
or Pineapple Filling
Confectioners sugar (optional)

Preheat oven to 350°F. Grease bottom of 9-inch springform pan and set aside.

Combine crumbs and sugar in small bowl. Add melted butter and stir until blended. Press crumbs onto bottom of prepared pan.

Bake 10 minutes. Cool completely on wire rack.

To make filling, beat cream cheese and sugar in medium-size bowl with electric mixer until light and fluffy. Beat in flour. Add eggs and vanilla and beat until thoroughly blended. Carefully grease inside edge of pan above crust. Spoon half of batter over cooled crust. Spoon raspberry filling over batter and top with remaining batter. Cut through batter and filling with flat-bladed knife to create swirled effect.

Bake 60 to 65 minutes or until center is set and top is golden. Cool completely in pan on wire rack. Refrigerate until ready to serve.

To serve, run tip of sharp knife around inside edge of pan and release side of pan. Place cheesecake on serving plate. Dust top with confectioners sugar, if desired.

12 to 14 servings

EaSY POPPY CREAM CHEESECAKE

½ cup butter or margarine, softened
¼ cup sugar
1 egg yolk

¼ teaspoon salt
1 cup all-purpose flour

Filling:

2 packages (8 ounces each) cream
  cheese, softened
½ cup sugar
2 eggs

1 can Solo or 1 jar Baker Poppy
  Filling, divided
1 teaspoon grated lemon peel
1 tablespoon lemon juice

Topping:

⅓ cup raisins
2 tablespoons dark rum

1 cup heavy cream

Beat butter, sugar, egg yolk, and salt in medium-size bowl with electric mixer until very creamy. Stir in flour to make soft dough. Shape dough into flattened round, wrap in waxed paper or plastic wrap, and refrigerate 30 minutes.

Press dough onto bottom and halfway up side of 9-inch springform pan. Set aside. Preheat oven to 350°F.

To make filling, beat cream cheese and sugar in medium-size bowl with electric mixer until light and fluffy. Beat in eggs. Add half of poppy filling, lemon peel, and lemon juice, and beat until thoroughly blended. Pour into pastry-lined pan.

Bake 50 to 55 minutes or until center is set. Cool completely in pan on wire rack. Refrigerate in pan several hours or until well chilled.

To make topping, place raisins in bowl, add rum, and stir. Set aside. Whip cream with electric mixer until firm. Place remaining poppy filling in medium-size bowl and stir in reserved raisins and rum. Fold in whipped cream.

To serve, run tip of sharp knife around inside edge of pan. Remove side of pan and place cake on serving dish. Spread poppy cream topping over cheesecake. Refrigerate until ready to serve.

12 servings   *(see photo page 74)*

FRUIT TOWER

**1 box (22 ounces) pie crust
sticks (4 sticks) or 2 boxes
(11 ounces each) pie crust mix
1 package (3½ ounces) instant
vanilla pudding mix**

**1½ cups milk
3 cans Solo or 3 jars Baker Fruit
Filling (choose 3 different flavors)
Sweetened whipped cream
to decorate (optional)**

Preheat oven to 375°F.

Prepare pie crust according to package directions and divide into 6 equal-size portions. Roll out 1 piece of pastry on lightly floured surface to 10-inch round. Cut into 8- or 9-inch circle, using inverted cake pan as guide. Place on ungreased baking sheet and prick lightly with fork.

Bake 12 to 14 minutes or until golden. Remove from baking sheet and cool completely on wire rack. Repeat with remaining pastry to make 6 pastry circles.

Prepare pudding mix according to package directions, using 1½ cups milk. Refrigerate until well chilled.

To assemble, place 1 pastry circle on serving plate and spread with one-fourth of vanilla pudding. Spread ½ container fruit filling over pudding and top with second pastry circle. Spread ½ container different flavor fruit filling over and top with third pastry circle. Spread one-fourth of vanilla pudding over and top with ½ container third flavor fruit filling. Repeat with remaining pastry circles, using one-fourth of vanilla pudding and ½ container first flavor fruit filling for layer 4; ½ container second flavor fruit filling for layer 5; and ending with remaining one-fourth of vanilla pudding and ½ container third flavor fruit filling for layer 6. Refrigerate 3 to 4 hours or until well chilled. Decorate with piped whipped cream, if desired.

12 servings

STRAWBERRY-FILLED CREAM PUFFS

1 cup water	½ cup unsalted butter
1 tablespoon granulated sugar	1 cup all-purpose flour
½ teaspoon salt	4 eggs

Filling:

2 cups heavy cream	1 can Solo or 1 jar Baker Strawberry,
3 tablespoons confectioners sugar	Cherry, Raspberry, Apricot,
2 teaspoons vanilla or 1 teaspoon	or Pineapple Filling
almond extract	Confectioners sugar

Preheat oven to 375°F. Grease 2 baking sheets and set aside.

Place water, granulated sugar, salt, and butter in medium-size saucepan. Bring mixture to full boil over high heat. Remove pan from heat and add flour all at once, beating vigorously with wooden spoon until mixture forms ball. Let cool 5 minutes.

Beat in eggs, 1 at a time, beating well after each addition. Drop mixture by heaping tablespoonfuls in 12 large mounds onto prepared baking sheets about 3 inches apart. Swirl top of each mound with back of spoon.

Bake 45 minutes. Remove from oven and cut slit in side of each cream puff. Return to oven and bake 10 minutes. Remove from baking sheets and cool completely on wire racks.

To make filling, whip cream in medium-size bowl with electric mixer until soft peaks form. Add confectioners sugar and vanilla and whip until firm. Fold into strawberry filling. Cut tops off puffs and remove any soft dough. Fill bottom halves of puffs with strawberry cream. Replace tops and refrigerate until ready to serve. Dust with confectioners sugar just before serving.

12 cream puffs

SUGARY ALMOND TWISTS

Sugar for sprinkling   **1 can Solo Almond Paste**
1 package (17¼ ounces) frozen puff
    pastry sheets, thawed

Preheat oven to 375°F.

Sprinkle work surface lightly with sugar. Unfold 1 sheet of pastry and lay flat on sugared surface. Roll out to 12-inch square.

Divide almond paste in half. Set half of almond paste aside and break remainder of paste into small pieces. Dot over half of pastry sheet. Fold pastry in half over almond paste and roll out to 10 x 12-inch rectangle. Sprinkle lightly with sugar. Fold in half again and roll out to 10 x 12-inch rectangle.

Cut pastry in half to make 2 rectangles, each 5 x 12 inches. Cut each rectangle into 12 strips, 1 inch wide. Twist strips into corkscrew shape and place on ungreased baking sheets about 1 inch apart. Sprinkle lightly with additional sugar, if desired. Repeat with remaining pastry sheet and reserved almond paste.

Bake 18 to 22 minutes or until puffed and golden brown. Remove from baking sheets immediately and cool completely on wire racks.

48 twists

Variation: For a stronger almond flavor, use a whole can of almond paste with each sheet of puff pastry.

1: *Break almond paste into small pieces and dot over half the pastry.*

2: *Cut each pastry rectangle in twelve 1-inch-wide strips. Twist strips into corkscrew shapes.*

Easy PUFF PASTRY APPLE POCKETS

1 package (17¼ ounces) frozen puff
   pastry sheets, thawed
1 can Solo or 1 jar Baker
   Apple Filling
⅓ cup raisins

1 teaspoon cinnamon
½ teaspoon grated lemon peel
Milk for brushing
Sugar for sprinkling

Preheat oven to 400°F.

Sprinkle work surface lightly with flour. Unfold 1 sheet of pastry and lay flat on floured surface. Roll out to 10 x 15-inch rectangle. Cut into six 5-inch circles.

Combine apple filling, raisins, cinnamon, and lemon peel in small bowl. Spoon 1 heaping tablespoonful apple filling on each pastry circle, slightly off center. Brush pastry edges with milk and fold pastry over filling to make half-moon shape. Press edge of pastries with fork to seal and place on ungreased baking sheets. Brush tops with milk and sprinkle with sugar. Repeat with remaining sheet of pastry and apple filling.

Bake 18 to 22 minutes or until golden brown. Remove from baking sheets and cool on wire racks.

12 pockets   *(see photo page 91)*

SOLO MINI TARTS

1 package (3 ounces) cream cheese,
   softened
½ cup butter or margarine
1 cup all-purpose flour

1 can Solo or 1 jar Baker
   Filling (any flavor)
Sweetened whipped cream to serve
   (optional)

Preheat oven to 400°F. Beat cream cheese and butter in medium-size bowl with electric mixer until well blended. Stir in flour. Shape dough into 1-inch balls. Press balls into bottom and up side of ungreased 1¾-inch miniature muffin pans. Bake 15 minutes or until lightly browned. Cool in pans. When cool, remove tart shells from pans and spoon filling into shells. Top with dollop of whipped cream, if desired.

About 24 tarts

ALMOND APPLE TART

1½ cups all-purpose flour
3 tablespoons granulated sugar
¼ teaspoon salt

½ cup butter or margarine
1 egg, beaten

Filling:

5 tablespoons butter or
margarine, softened
2 eggs
1 teaspoon rum extract or
brandy extract

1 can Solo or 1 jar Baker
Almond Filling
1 can Solo or 1 jar Baker
Apple Filling

To Decorate:

¾ cup heavy cream
1 tablespoon confectioners sugar

¼ cup toasted sliced almonds

Stir flour, granulated sugar, and salt in medium-size bowl until blended. Cut in butter until mixture resembles coarse crumbs. Add egg and mix until dough binds together. Press into bottom and up side of 9- or 10-inch fluted tart pan with removable bottom. Trim pastry even with rim of pan. Refrigerate 30 minutes.

Preheat oven to 375°F.

To make filling, beat butter in medium-size bowl until fluffy. Add eggs and rum extract, and beat with electric mixer until blended. Beat in almond filling until thoroughly blended. Spread apple filling in bottom of pastry-lined pan. Pour almond mixture evenly over filling.

Bake 40 to 45 minutes or until center is set and pastry is golden brown. Cool completely in pan on wire rack.

To decorate, whip cream in medium-size bowl with electric mixer until soft peaks form. Add confectioners sugar and whip until firm. Spoon whipped cream into pastry bag fitted with open star tip. Pipe on top of tart in decorative swirls. Sprinkle with toasted almonds and refrigerate until ready to serve.

10 to 12 servings   *(see photo page 86)*

Cakes –
Simple
to
Elegant

Blitz Torte (page 103)

APRICOT RUM GÂTEAU

3 eggs
1 cup sugar
1½ cups cake flour
1½ teaspoons baking powder

½ teaspoon salt
⅔ cup warm milk
2 tablespoons butter,
    melted and cooled

Syrup:
½ cup sugar
1 cup water

½ cup dark rum

Custard Filling:
2 tablespoons cornstarch
⅓ cup sugar
¼ teaspoon salt

1 cup milk
2 egg yolks, beaten
1 teaspoon vanilla or rum extract

Topping:
1 can Solo or 1 jar Baker
    Apricot Filling

To Decorate:
½ cup slivered toasted almonds
    (optional)

1 cup sweetened whipped cream

Preheat oven to 350°F. Grease three 9-inch round cake pans. Line bottoms of pans with parchment paper or waxed paper. Grease paper and set aside.

Beat eggs and sugar in medium-size bowl with electric mixer until thick and lemon-colored, about 5 minutes. Sift flour, baking powder, and salt gradually over egg mixture and fold in. Add milk and melted butter and mix until smooth. Divide batter and spread evenly in prepared pans.

Bake 35 minutes or until centers spring back when lightly pressed. Cool in pans on wire racks 10 minutes. Remove from pans and peel off lining paper.

To make syrup, place sugar and water in small saucepan. Bring to a boil over high heat, stirring constantly, until sugar is dissolved. Boil rapidly 3 to 5 minutes or until mixture is consistency of thin syrup. Remove from heat and cool slightly. Stir in rum.

Place warm cake layers in deep plates. Pierce with prongs of fork or skewer. Pour syrup evenly over each layer and let stand until syrup is absorbed.

To make filling, stir cornstarch, sugar, and salt in medium-size saucepan. Add milk and stir until mixture is blended and smooth. Cook over low heat, stirring, until mixture thickens. Stir 3 tablespoons hot milk mixture slowly into beaten egg yolks. Return mixture to saucepan and cook, stirring constantly, until mixture thickens and coats back of spoon. Pour into bowl and stir in vanilla. Press sheet of waxed paper over surface of custard to prevent skin from forming. Refrigerate until custard is chilled.

To assemble, place 1 rum-soaked layer on serving plate and spread with half of chilled custard. Top with second layer and spread with remaining custard. Top with third layer. Spread apricot filling over top and around side of cake. Lightly press toasted almonds around side of cake, if desired. Spoon whipped cream into pastry bag fitted with open star tip and pipe in lattice pattern on top of cake. Refrigerate until ready to serve.

12 to 14 servings

BLITZ TORTE

½ cup butter or margarine, softened
½ cup granulated sugar
4 egg yolks
¼ cup milk

1 teaspoon vanilla
1 cup sifted cake flour
1½ teaspoons baking powder
¼ teaspoon salt

Meringue Topping:
4 egg whites
⅛ teaspoon salt
1 cup granulated sugar

1 teaspoon vanilla
¼ cup finely chopped pecans

Filling:
1 cup heavy cream
2 tablespoons confectioners sugar

1 can Solo or 1 jar Baker Apricot, Raspberry, Strawberry, Pineapple, or Cherry Filling

Preheat oven to 350°F. Grease and flour two 9-inch round cake pans and set aside.

Beat butter and granulated sugar in medium-size bowl with electric mixer until light and fluffy. Beat in egg yolks, 1 at a time, beating well after each addition. Add milk and vanilla and beat until blended. Stir flour, baking powder, and salt until mixed. Add to butter mixture and beat 2 minutes on high speed. Spread batter evenly in prepared pans. Set aside.

To make meringue topping, beat egg whites and salt in medium-size bowl with electric mixer until soft peaks form. Add granulated sugar, 2 tablespoons at a time, beating well after each addition. Add vanilla and beat until stiff and glossy. Spread meringue evenly over layers, making sure meringue touches edge of pans all the way around. Sprinkle pecans over 1 layer.

Bake 30 to 35 minutes or until cake tester inserted in center comes out clean. Cool completely in pans on wire racks. Remove layers from pans carefully, meringue side up.

To make filling, whip cream in medium-size bowl with electric mixer until soft peaks form. Add confectioners sugar and whip until firm. Fold into apricot filling.

To assemble, place plain meringue layer, meringue side up, on serving plate. Spread with one-third of apricot cream filling. Place nut-covered meringue layer on top, nut side up. Spread remaining apricot cream around side of torte. Refrigerate until ready to serve.

10 to 12 servings   *(see photo pages 100-101)*

SOLO POPPY CAKE

1 cup butter or margarine, softened	1 cup dairy sour cream
1½ cups sugar	2½ cups all-purpose flour
1 can Solo or 1 jar Baker	1 teaspoon baking soda
Poppy Filling	1 teaspoon salt
4 eggs, separated	Confectioners sugar
1 teaspoon vanilla	

Preheat oven to 350°F. Grease and flour 12-cup Bundt pan or 10-inch tube pan and set aside.

Beat butter and sugar in large bowl with electric mixer until light and fluffy. Add poppy filling and beat until blended. Beat in egg yolks, 1 at a time, beating well after each addition. Add vanilla and sour cream and beat just until blended. Stir flour, baking soda, and salt until mixed, and add to poppy mixture gradually, beating well after each addition.

Beat egg whites in separate bowl with electric mixer until stiff peaks form. Fold beaten egg whites into batter. Spread batter evenly in prepared pan.

Bake 50 to 60 minutes or until cake tester inserted in center comes out clean. Cool in pan on wire rack 10 minutes. Remove from pan and cool completely on rack. Dust with confectioners sugar just before serving.

14 to 16 servings

Easy

ALMOND CAKE

1 cup butter or margarine, softened	2¼ cups all-purpose flour
1 cup granulated sugar	2 teaspoons baking powder
3 eggs	½ teaspoon salt
1 can Solo or 1 jar Baker	¼ cup milk
Almond Filling	

Almond Glaze:

1 cup confectioners sugar	¼ teaspoon almond extract
2 tablespoons light cream	

Preheat oven to 350°F. Grease and flour 10-inch tube pan or 12-cup Bundt pan and set aside.

Beat butter and granulated sugar in large bowl with electric mixer until light and fluffy. Add eggs, 1 at a time, beating well after each addition. Beat in almond filling until blended. Stir flour, baking powder, and salt until mixed. Add to almond mixture alternately with milk, beginning and ending with dry ingredients. Beat until blended. Spread batter evenly in prepared pan.

Bake 50 to 55 minutes or until cake tester inserted in center comes out clean. Cool in pan on wire rack 10 minutes. Remove from pan and cool completely on rack.

To make glaze, combine confectioners sugar, cream, and almond extract in small bowl, and stir until blended and smooth. Spoon or drizzle over top of cake. Let stand until glaze is set.

10 to 12 servings

Solo Poppy Cake (opposite)

VIENNESE POPPY CAKE

¾ cup cake flour
½ teaspoon baking powder
½ teaspoon salt
½ cup raisins, finely chopped
½ cup butter or margarine, softened

¾ cup granulated sugar, divided
6 eggs, separated
1 can Solo or 1 jar Baker
    Poppy Filling
¼ cup dark rum

Chocolate Glaze:

2 squares (2 ounces) unsweetened
    chocolate, chopped
2 tablespoons unsalted butter
1 tablespoon light corn syrup

2 tablespoons dark rum
1 tablespoon warm water
1 cup confectioners sugar

Preheat oven to 350°F. Grease 9-inch springform pan and line bottom of pan with parchment paper or waxed paper. Grease paper and set aside.

Sift flour, baking powder, and salt into small bowl. Add raisins and toss to coat. Set aside.

Beat butter and ½ cup granulated sugar in large bowl with electric mixer until light and fluffy. Add egg yolks, 2 at a time, beating well after each addition. Add poppy filling and rum and beat until blended. Fold in flour-raisin mixture.

Beat egg whites in separate bowl with electric mixer until soft peaks form. Add remaining ¼ cup granulated sugar gradually and beat until stiff peaks form. Stir one-third of beaten egg whites into poppy seed mixture to lighten. Fold in remaining egg whites. Spread batter evenly in prepared pan.

Bake 40 to 45 minutes or until cake tester inserted in center comes out clean. Cool in pan on wire rack 10 minutes. Remove from pan, peel off lining paper, and cool completely on rack.

To make glaze, melt chocolate, butter, and corn syrup in small saucepan over low heat, stirring constantly until smooth. Cook 1 minute and remove from heat. Add rum, water, and confectioners sugar. Beat vigorously until glaze is smooth and glossy. Line edge of serving plate with strips of waxed paper. Place cake on serving plate and pour glaze over. Spread evenly over top and around side of cake. Remove waxed paper carefully and let stand until glaze is set.

10 to 12 servings   *(see photo page 119)*

Note: Flavor of cake will be enhanced if cake is wrapped and set aside overnight before it is glazed.

CHERRY SPONGE TORTE

4 eggs, separated
¼ cup warm water
¾ cup granulated sugar

1 teaspoon vanilla
1¼ cups sifted cake flour
2 teaspoons baking powder

Custard Filling:
⅓ cup granulated sugar
¼ cup all-purpose flour
1 cup milk
2 egg yolks, beaten

1 teaspoon vanilla
1 can Solo or 1 jar Baker
     Cherry Filling

To Decorate (optional):
¾ cup heavy cream

2 tablespoons confectioners sugar

Preheat oven to 350°F. Grease two 9-inch round cake pans and line bottoms of pans with parchment paper or waxed paper. Grease paper and set aside.

Beat egg yolks and warm water in large bowl with electric mixer until foamy. Add granulated sugar and vanilla and beat until thick and pale yellow. Stir flour and baking powder and fold into egg yolk mixture. Beat egg whites with electric mixer until stiff peaks form. Fold into egg yolk mixture. Spread batter evenly in prepared pans.

Bake 25 to 30 minutes or until centers spring back when lightly pressed. Cool in pans on wire racks 10 minutes. Remove from pans, peel off lining paper, and cool completely on racks.

To make custard filling, stir granulated sugar and flour in medium-size saucepan until mixed. Stir milk in slowly, stirring constantly, until mixture is smooth. Cook over low heat, stirring, until mixture thickens and just comes to a boil. Add about ¼ cup hot milk mixture very slowly to beaten egg yolks, stirring constantly, until blended. Pour back into saucepan and cook, stirring, until custard coats back of spoon. Pour into bowl and stir in vanilla. Set aside to cool. Press sheet of waxed paper over surface of custard to prevent skin from forming, and refrigerate 1 hour.

To assemble cake, place 1 cake layer upside down on serving plate and spread with custard filling. Top with remaining cake layer. Spread cherry filling over top of cake to edges all the way around. Refrigerate 2 hours.

If desired, beat cream in medium-size bowl with electric mixer until soft peaks form. Add confectioners sugar and beat until firm. Spread whipped cream around side of cake. Refrigerate until ready to serve.

8 to 10 servings

MARZIPAN STRAWBERRY CAKE

6 eggs
1 can Solo Almond Paste
1 teaspoon almond extract
½ cup sugar
½ cup plus 2 tablespoons cake flour

1 teaspoon baking powder
1 cup Solo Strawberry or
   Peach Glaze
Strawberries or sliced peaches
   to decorate

Preheat oven to 350°F. Grease and flour 10-inch tube pan and set aside. Separate eggs and set egg whites aside to come to room temperature.

Beat egg yolks in large bowl with electric mixer until thick and lemon-colored. Add about one-third of almond paste at a time, breaking it into small pieces and beating well after each addition until smooth. Beat in almond extract. Set aside.

Beat egg whites in large bowl with electric mixer until soft peaks form. Add sugar gradually, 2 tablespoons at a time, and beat until stiff and glossy. Stir one-third of beaten egg whites into egg yolk mixture to lighten. Fold in remaining egg whites. Sift flour and baking powder over batter and fold in just until blended. Spread batter evenly in prepared pan.

Bake 30 to 35 minutes or until cake tester inserted in center comes out clean. Cool in pan on wire rack 15 minutes. Remove from pan and cool completely on rack.

Cut cake into 2 layers. Place bottom layer on serving plate, cut side up, and spread half of strawberry glaze over. Place second layer on top and spread with remaining glaze. Decorate with strawberries.

10 to 12 servings

APRICOT SACHER TORTE

¾ cup unsalted butter, softened
⅔ cup granulated sugar
7 eggs, separated
6 ounces top-quality semisweet
   chocolate, melted and cooled
1 teaspoon vanilla

½ cup Solo Toasted Almond
   Crunch Topping
1 cup sifted cake flour
1 can Solo or 1 jar Baker
   Apricot Filling

Glaze:

2 ounces top-quality unsweetened
   chocolate, coarsely chopped
4 to 5 tablespoons light cream or
   half and half

2 tablespoons light corn syrup
2 cups sifted confectioners sugar

Preheat oven to 325°F. Grease and flour 9-inch springform pan and set aside.

Beat butter and granulated sugar in large bowl with electric mixer until light and fluffy. Add egg yolks, 1 at a time, beating well after each addition. Add melted chocolate and vanilla and beat until blended. Stir in toasted almond crunch topping. Fold flour in gradually.

Beat egg whites in large bowl with electric mixer until stiff peaks form. Stir one-third of egg whites into chocolate mixture to lighten. Fold in remaining egg whites. Pour into prepared pan.

Bake 40 to 45 minutes or until center springs back when lightly pressed. Cool in pan on wire rack 10 minutes. Remove side of pan and cool completely on rack.

Cut cake into 2 layers. Place bottom layer on serving plate and spread one-third of apricot filling over. Replace top layer and spread remaining apricot filling over top and around side of cake. Let stand until firm.

To make glaze, place chocolate, 4 tablespoons cream, and corn syrup in medium-size saucepan. Cook over low heat, stirring, until chocolate is melted and mixture is smooth. Add confectioners sugar and beat vigorously with wooden spoon until mixture is smooth and glaze is thin enough to pour. Add additional cream if necessary. Remove from heat and set aside to cool slightly. Pour over cake and spread evenly. Let stand until glaze is set.

10 to 12 servings

RASPBERRY PECAN TORTE

½ cup butter or margarine, softened
1 cup granulated sugar
2 eggs
1 teaspoon vanilla
1 cup all-purpose flour

1½ teaspoons baking powder
½ teaspoon salt
⅓ cup milk
½ cup ground pecans

Filling:
½ cup butter or margarine, softened
1½ cups sifted confectioners sugar
1 egg

1 can Solo or 1 jar Baker Raspberry, Strawberry, or Cherry Filling

Topping:
¾ cup heavy cream
2 to 3 tablespoons confectioners sugar

½ cup finely chopped pecans

Preheat oven to 350°F. Grease and flour 9-inch square baking pan and set aside.

Beat butter and granulated sugar in medium-size bowl with electric mixer until light and fluffy. Add eggs and vanilla and beat until blended. Stir flour, baking powder, and salt until mixed. Add to butter mixture alternately with milk, beating until blended. Fold in ground pecans and spread batter in prepared pan.

Bake 30 to 35 minutes or until center springs back when lightly pressed. Cool in pan on wire rack 5 minutes. Remove from pan and cool completely on rack.

To make filling, beat butter and confectioners sugar in medium-size bowl with electric mixer until light and fluffy. Add egg and beat until blended.

Cut cake in half horizontally to make 2 layers. Place 1 layer on serving plate and spread with butter filling. Cover with raspberry filling and top with second layer.

To make topping, whip cream in medium-size bowl with electric mixer until soft peaks form. Add confectioners sugar and whip until firm. Fold in chopped pecans.

Spread over top of torte. Refrigerate at least 3 to 4 hours. Cut into nine 3-inch squares.

9 squares

SPECIAL OCCASION MARZIPAN CAKE

1 cup butter or margarine, softened
2 cups granulated sugar
5 eggs
2 teaspoons vanilla

3½ cups sifted cake flour
1½ teaspoons baking powder
1 teaspoon salt
¾ cup milk

Filling and Marzipan Layer:

¾ cup heavy cream
1 can Solo or 1 jar Baker
   Raspberry Filling, divided
2 tablespoons lemon juice

3 tablespoons water
Confectioners sugar
½ recipe Marzipan, tinted if desired
   (page 144)

Icing:

2 egg whites
⅛ teaspoon cream of tartar
½ teaspoon lemon juice

2½ cups sifted confectioners sugar
Food coloring (optional)

Preheat oven to 350°F. Grease 10-inch springform pan or 10 x 3-inch-deep cake pan. Line bottom of pan with parchment paper or waxed paper. Grease paper and set aside.

Beat butter and granulated sugar in large bowl with electric mixer until light and fluffy. Add eggs, 1 at a time, beating well after each addition. Beat in vanilla. Stir flour, baking powder, and salt until mixed. Add to butter mixture alternately with milk, beginning and ending with dry ingredients. Spread batter evenly in prepared pan.

Bake 60 to 70 minutes or until cake tester inserted in center comes out clean. Cool in pan on wire rack 10 minutes. Remove from pan, peel off lining paper, and cool completely on rack.

To make filling, whip cream in medium-size bowl with electric mixer until firm. Set aside ¼ cup raspberry filling. Fold whipped cream into remaining raspberry filling and chill 2 hours.

Cut cake in half horizontally to make 2 layers. Place bottom layer on cake stand or flat plate. Spread raspberry cream filling over bottom layer and top with second layer. Press down gently and scrape off any excess filling around side of cake to make perfectly smooth surface.

To make marzipan layer, place reserved ¼ cup raspberry filling, lemon juice, and water in small saucepan. Cook over medium heat, stirring, until mixture comes to a boil. Boil 2 to 3 minutes or until syrupy. Press raspberry syrup through strainer to remove seeds, and let cool slightly. Brush syrup over top and around side of cake, covering cake completely.

Sprinkle work surface and rolling pin with confectioners sugar. Roll out marzipan on sugared surface to 15-inch circle. Roll marzipan around rolling pin to prevent it from tearing. Drape over cake and use rolling pin on top of cake to make smooth surface. Press marzipan over edge and around side of cake with small, thin spatula. Trim bottom edge of marzipan with sharp knife or scissors. Reserve trimmings for decorations, if desired. Smooth any cracks or folds with fingertips and set cake aside.

To make icing, beat egg whites and cream of tartar in medium-size bowl with electric mixer until foamy. Add lemon juice and confectioners sugar gradually, beating constantly at high speed until icing is thick and glossy. Beat until icing is very stiff and stands in stiff, sharp peaks when beaters are lifted. Beat in food coloring, if desired, 1 drop at a time. Cover bowl of icing with damp cloth while frosting cake to prevent crust from forming on surface of icing.

Spread very thin layer of icing over top and around side of cake, smoothing icing with icing spatula. Let stand several hours or until icing is dry. Spread second thin layer of icing over cake. Spoon small amount of icing into pastry bag fitted with plain or open star tip and pipe decoratively on top and around side of cake. Tint reserved marzipan and decorate cake with marzipan leaves and flowers, if desired.

12 to 16 servings

BUTTERMILK PRUNE CAKE

½ cup butter or margarine, softened
½ cup granulated sugar
½ cup firmly packed brown sugar
3 eggs
1 teaspoon vanilla
1 can Solo or 1 jar Baker
  Prune Filling

2¼ cups all-purpose flour
1 teaspoon baking soda
1 teaspoon baking powder
1 teaspoon salt
1 cup buttermilk
1 cup chopped walnuts, pecans,
  or almonds

Nutty Frosting:
⅓ cup butter or margarine
¼ cup heavy cream
½ cup firmly packed brown sugar

¾ cup chopped walnuts, pecans,
  or almonds

Preheat oven to 325°F. Grease and flour 10-inch tube pan and set aside.

Beat butter and sugars in large bowl with electric mixer until light and fluffy. Add eggs and vanilla and beat until blended. Beat in prune filling.

Stir flour, baking soda, baking powder, and salt until mixed. Add to butter mixture alternately with buttermilk, beating until blended and beginning and ending with dry ingredients. Fold in chopped nuts. Spread evenly in prepared pan.

Bake 65 to 75 minutes or until cake tester inserted in center comes out clean. Cool in pan on wire rack 15 minutes. Remove from pan and cool completely on rack.

To make frosting, place butter, cream, and brown sugar in medium-size saucepan. Cook over medium heat, stirring, until butter is melted. Stir in nuts. Reduce heat and cook 4 minutes. Preheat broiler. Spread warm frosting over top of cake. Place cake on rack in broiler pan about 4 inches from source of heat. Broil 2 minutes (do not allow frosting to burn). Remove cake to wire rack and let cool completely.

12 to 16 servings

APPLE GINGER CAKE

2 eggs
1½ cups granulated sugar
½ cup vegetable oil
2 teaspoons vanilla
1 can Solo or 1 jar Baker
    Apple Filling
2 cups all-purpose flour

2 teaspoons baking soda
2 teaspoons ground ginger
1 teaspoon cinnamon
1 teaspoon salt
½ teaspoon nutmeg
1 cup chopped walnuts or pecans

Cream Cheese Frosting:

2 packages (3 ounces each) cream
    cheese, softened
1 teaspoon vanilla
4 cups sifted confectioners sugar

2 to 3 tablespoons milk or
    half and half
1 to 2 teaspoons cinnamon
    (optional)

Preheat oven to 350°F. Grease 10-inch tube pan or fluted cake pan and set aside.

Beat eggs, granulated sugar, oil, and vanilla in large bowl with electric mixer until blended. Stir in apple filling. Sift flour, baking soda, ginger, cinnamon, salt, and nutmeg. Add to apple mixture and stir until blended. Fold in nuts and spread batter evenly in prepared pan.

Bake 60 to 65 minutes or until cake tester inserted in center comes out clean. Cool in pan on wire rack 15 minutes. Remove from pan and cool completely on wire rack.

To make frosting, beat cream cheese in medium-size bowl with electric mixer until creamy. Add vanilla, confectioners sugar, and 2 tablespoons milk. Beat until frosting is fluffy and of good spreading consistency, adding remaining milk only if necessary. Beat in cinnamon, if desired. Spread frosting over top and around side of cake. Refrigerate 1 hour before serving.

10 to 12 servings

Easy QUICK SOLO POPPY CAKE

1 package (18¼ ounces) yellow cake
    mix (traditional or
    pudding-included)
3 eggs
⅓ cup vegetable oil

¼ cup water
1 cup dairy sour cream
1 can Solo or 1 jar Baker
    Poppy Filling

Preheat oven to 350°F. Grease and flour 12-cup Bundt pan or 9 x 13-inch baking pan and set aside.

Place cake mix, eggs, oil, water, sour cream, and poppy filling in large bowl and beat on low speed with electric mixer until well blended. Increase speed to high and beat 2 minutes. Pour into prepared pan and smooth top.

Bake 55 to 65 minutes for Bundt cake (50 to 60 minutes for 9 x 13-inch cake) or until cake tester inserted in center comes out clean. Cool Bundt cake in pan on wire rack 15 minutes. Remove from pan and cool completely on rack. Cool oblong cake completely in pan on wire rack.

16 to 20 servings

Apple Ginger Cake (opposite), Date Orange Cake (page 120)

PECAN COCONUT CAKE

1 cup quick-cooking rolled oats	1 can Solo Pecan Filling
1 cup flaked or shredded coconut	2¼ cups all-purpose flour
1 cup raisins	2 teaspoons baking powder
1 cup butter or margarine, softened	½ teaspoon cinnamon
1 cup sugar	¼ teaspoon salt
3 eggs	½ cup milk
1 teaspoon vanilla	Confectioners sugar

Preheat oven to 350°F. Grease 12-cup Bundt pan and set aside.

Combine oats, coconut, and raisins in medium-size bowl and set aside.

Beat butter and sugar in large bowl with electric mixer until light and fluffy. Add eggs and vanilla and beat until blended. Beat in pecan filling. Stir flour, baking powder, cinnamon, and salt until mixed. Add to butter mixture alternately with milk, beginning and ending with dry ingredients. Beat until well blended. Fold in reserved oat mixture. Spread batter evenly in prepared pan.

Bake 55 to 60 minutes or until cake tester inserted in center comes out clean. Cool in pan on wire rack 15 minutes. Remove from pan and cool completely on rack. Dust with confectioners sugar before serving.

12 to 16 servings

Easy   ANISETTE POPPY CAKE

1 package (18¼ ounces) pudding-included butter flavor cake mix	½ cup anisette liqueur*
4 eggs	¼ cup warm water
½ cup butter or margarine, softened	1 can Solo or 1 jar Baker Poppy Filling

Glaze:

1 cup confectioners sugar	1 tablespoon milk or water
2 tablespoons anisette liqueur	

Preheat oven to 325°F. Grease and flour 12-cup Bundt pan or 10-inch tube pan and set aside.

Place cake mix, eggs, butter, anisette liqueur, warm water, and poppy filling in large bowl and beat at low speed with electric mixer until well blended. Increase speed to high and beat 2 minutes. Spread batter evenly in prepared pan.

Bake 45 to 50 minutes or until cake tester inserted in center comes out clean. Cool in pan on wire rack 15 minutes. Remove from pan and cool completely on rack.

To make glaze, combine confectioners sugar, anisette liqueur, and milk in small bowl and stir until smooth. Spoon or drizzle glaze over cooled cake. Let stand until glaze is set.

12 to 16 servings

*Note: To replace anisette liqueur, use 2 teaspoons anise extract stirred into ½ cup water in cake batter. For glaze, use 1 teaspoon anise extract and increase milk to 3 tablespoons.

ALMOND SPICE CAKE

6 eggs, separated
1 cup granulated sugar, divided
2 tablespoons vegetable oil
1 teaspoon almond extract or
   1 tablespoon almond-
   flavored liqueur
¼ cup all-purpose flour
1 teaspoon baking powder

1 teaspoon cinnamon
½ teaspoon nutmeg
½ teaspoon allspice
1 can Solo Toasted Almond
   Crunch Topping
½ cup chopped almonds or
   pecans (optional)

Frosting:

½ cup butter or margarine, softened
1 teaspoon almond extract
1 box (16 ounces) confectioners
   sugar, sifted

3 to 4 tablespoons milk or almond-
   flavored liqueur

Preheat oven to 350°F. Grease two 9-inch round cake pans and line bottoms of pans with parchment paper or waxed paper. Grease paper and set aside.

Beat egg yolks and ½ cup granulated sugar in large bowl with electric mixer until thickened and pale yellow, about 5 minutes. Add oil and almond extract and beat until blended. Stir flour, baking powder, cinnamon, nutmeg, and allspice until mixed. Add to egg yolk mixture and beat until blended.

Beat egg whites in separate bowl with electric mixer until soft peaks form. Add remaining ½ cup granulated sugar gradually and beat until stiff and glossy.

Stir 3 heaping tablespoons beaten egg whites into egg yolk mixture to lighten. Fold in remaining egg whites, toasted almond crunch topping, and chopped nuts, if desired. Spread batter evenly in prepared pans.

Bake 30 to 35 minutes or until centers spring back when lightly pressed. Cool in pans on wire racks 10 minutes. Remove from pans, peel off lining paper, and cool completely on racks.

To make frosting, beat butter in medium-size bowl with electric mixer until creamy. Add almond extract, confectioners sugar, and milk, and beat until frosting is fluffy and of good spreading consistency.

Place 1 cake layer, bottom side up, on serving plate. Spread with one-third of frosting. Place second layer on top and spread remaining frosting over top and around side of cake.

8 to 12 servings

DATE NUT CAKE

1 can Solo or 1 jar Baker
  Date Filling
½ cup water
¼ cup butter or margarine, softened
1 cup sugar
1 teaspoon vanilla
1 egg

1⅔ cups all-purpose flour
1 teaspoon baking soda
½ teaspoon salt
½ cup chopped walnuts, pecans,
  or almonds
Sweetened whipped cream
  to serve (optional)

Preheat oven to 350°F. Grease and flour 9-inch square baking pan and set aside.
Combine date filling and water in small bowl and stir until blended. Set aside.
Beat butter and sugar in medium-size bowl with electric mixer until light and fluffy. Add vanilla and egg and beat until blended. Stir flour, baking soda, and salt until mixed, and add to butter mixture alternately with date mixture, beginning and ending with dry ingredients. Beat until smooth. Stir in chopped walnuts. Spread batter evenly in prepared pan.
Bake 50 to 60 minutes or until cake tester inserted in center comes out clean. Cool completely in pan on wire rack. Cut into nine 3-inch squares and serve with whipped cream, if desired.

9 squares

PINEAPPLE CRUNCH CAKE

2¼ cups cake flour
2½ teaspoons baking powder
1 teaspoon salt
½ cup butter or margarine
1¼ cups granulated sugar
3 eggs

1 can Solo or 1 jar Baker Pineapple
  Filling or any flavor Fruit
  Filling, divided
1 teaspoon vanilla
¾ cup milk
½ cup Solo Toasted Almond Crunch
  Topping, divided

Frosting:

6 tablespoons butter or margarine
3 cups sifted confectioners sugar

1 teaspoon rum extract or vanilla
2 to 3 tablespoons milk

Preheat oven to 350°F. Grease and flour two 9-inch round cake pans and set aside.
Sift flour, baking powder, and salt onto sheet of waxed paper and set aside.
Beat butter and granulated sugar in large bowl with electric mixer until light and fluffy. Add eggs and beat until blended. Beat in ⅓ cup pineapple filling and vanilla. Add flour alternately with milk, beating well after each addition, beginning and ending with dry ingredients. Divide batter and spread evenly in prepared pans.

Bake 30 to 35 minutes or until cake tester inserted in center comes out clean. Cool in pans on wire racks 10 minutes. Remove from pans and cool completely on racks.

Place 1 cake layer, bottom side up, on serving plate and spread remaining pineapple filling over. Sprinkle ¼ cup almond crunch topping over pineapple filling and top with second layer.

To make frosting, beat butter in medium-size bowl with electric mixer until creamy. Add confectioners sugar, rum extract, and milk. Beat until frosting is fluffy and of good spreading consistency. Spread over top and around side of cake, swirling frosting with back of metal spoon. Sprinkle remaining ¼ cup toasted almond crunch topping over top of cake.

8 to 12 servings

NUTTY ORANGE CAKE

1 cup butter or margarine, softened	1 teaspoon grated lemon peel
1¼ cups sugar	2½ cups all-purpose flour
3 eggs	2 teaspoons baking powder
1 can Solo or 1 jar Baker	1 teaspoon baking soda
Nut Filling, or 1 can	½ teaspoon salt
Solo Pecan Filling	1 cup orange juice
1 teaspoon grated orange peel	

Orange Rum Sauce:

¾ cup orange juice	¾ cup sugar
2 tablespoons lemon juice	¼ cup dark rum

Preheat oven to 350°F. Grease and flour 10-inch tube pan or 12-cup Bundt pan and set aside.

Beat butter and sugar in large bowl with electric mixer until light and fluffy. Add eggs, 1 at a time, beating well after each addition. Add nut filling, orange peel, and lemon peel, and beat until blended. Sift flour, baking powder, baking soda, and salt. Add to butter mixture alternately with orange juice, beginning and ending with dry ingredients. Spread batter evenly in prepared pan.

Bake 55 to 60 minutes or until cake tester inserted in center comes out clean. Cool in pan on wire rack 15 minutes. Remove from pan and place on rack.

To make sauce, place orange juice, lemon juice, and sugar in small saucepan and stir to combine. Cook over medium heat, stirring occasionally, until mixture comes to a boil and sugar is dissolved. Reduce heat and cook 10 minutes. Remove from heat and cool 5 minutes. Stir in rum. Place warm cake on serving plate and prick with fork. Spoon sauce over cake and let stand until liquid is absorbed.

12 to 14 servings

Variation: Dust cake with confectioners sugar instead of using Orange Rum Sauce.

CHERRY CREAM NUT ROLL

5 eggs, separated
½ cup granulated sugar
1 teaspoon brandy extract or
    rum extract
1 can Solo or 1 jar Baker Nut Filling

½ cup all-purpose flour
½ teaspoon baking powder
¼ teaspoon salt
Confectioners sugar

Filling:

2 cups heavy cream
3 to 4 tablespoons confectioners
    sugar

1½ teaspoons brandy extract or
    rum extract
1 can Solo or 1 jar Baker
    Cherry Filling

Preheat oven to 350°F. Grease 15 x 10-inch jelly-roll pan. Line pan with waxed paper. Grease paper and set aside.

Beat egg yolks and granulated sugar about 5 minutes in large bowl with electric mixer until thick and pale yellow. Beat in brandy extract and nut filling until well blended.

Beat egg whites in separate bowl with electric mixer until stiff peaks form. Stir 3 heaping tablespoons egg whites into nut mixture to lighten. Fold in remaining egg whites. Sift flour, baking powder, and salt over nut mixture and fold in. Spread batter evenly in prepared pan.

Bake 20 to 22 minutes or until center springs back when lightly pressed.

Sprinkle towel with confectioners sugar. Invert cake onto sugared towel and remove pan. Peel off lining paper and trim off any crusty edges. Roll up cake and towel, jelly-roll style, starting from short side. Place on wire rack and cool completely.

To fill cake, unroll cooled cake on flat surface. Whip cream in large bowl with electric mixer until soft peaks form. Add confectioners sugar and brandy extract and whip until firm. Fold whipped cream into cherry filling. Spread half of cherry cream over cake. Reroll cake without towel and place, seam side down, on serving plate. Spread remaining cherry cream over side and top of cake. Refrigerate until ready to serve.

8 to 10 servings

Cherry Cream Nut Roll (opposite), Viennese Poppy Cake (page 106)

Easy   FUZZY NAVEL CAKE

1 package (18¼ ounces) orange or
　　yellow cake mix
3 eggs
½ cup orange juice
½ cup peach schnapps liqueur

1 jar Baker Peach or Apricot Filling
　　or 1 can Solo Apricot Filling
2 teaspoons grated orange peel
　　(optional)

Glaze:

1 cup confectioners sugar

3 tablespoons peach schnapps
　　liqueur

Preheat oven to 350°F. Grease 12-cup Bundt pan or 10-inch tube pan and set aside.

Place cake mix, eggs, orange juice, peach schnapps, peach filling, and orange peel in large bowl. Beat at low speed with electric mixer until well blended. Increase speed to high and beat 2 minutes. Spread batter evenly in prepared pan.

Bake 50 to 60 minutes or until cake tester inserted in center comes out clean. Cool in pan on wire rack 20 minutes. Remove from pan and cool completely on rack.

To make glaze, combine confectioners sugar and peach schnapps in small bowl and stir until smooth. Spoon or drizzle glaze over cooled cake. Let stand until glaze is set.

12 to 16 servings

DATE ORANGE CAKE

½ cup butter or margarine, softened
1 cup granulated sugar
2 eggs
2 teaspoons grated orange peel
1 can Solo or 1 jar Baker
　　Date Filling, divided

2 cups all-purpose flour
2 teaspoons baking powder
½ teaspoon baking soda
½ teaspoon salt
1 cup orange juice
½ cup chopped pecans or walnuts

Orange Glaze:

1 cup confectioners sugar
2 to 3 tablespoons orange juice

½ teaspoon grated orange
　　peel (optional)

Preheat oven to 350°F. Grease and flour 13 x 9-inch baking pan and set aside.

Beat butter and granulated sugar in medium-size bowl with electric mixer until light and fluffy. Add eggs and orange peel and beat until blended. Beat in half of date filling. Stir flour, baking powder, baking soda, and salt until mixed. Add to butter mixture alternately with orange juice, beginning and ending with dry ingredients. Beat until well blended. Fold in pecans and spread batter evenly in prepared pan. Spoon remaining date filling into 12 mounds on top of batter. Swirl date filling lightly through batter with flat-bladed knife.

Bake 45 to 50 minutes or until cake tester inserted in center comes out clean. Cool completely in pan on wire rack.

To make glaze, combine confectioners sugar and orange juice in small bowl and stir until smooth. Stir in orange peel. Spoon or drizzle over cooled cake. Let stand until glaze is set.

12 servings   *(see photo page 112)*

Easy SNACKIN' DATE CAKE

¼ cup butter or margarine, softened
⅔ cup granulated sugar
1 egg
1 teaspoon vanilla

1 can Solo or 1 jar Baker
  Date Filling
1¾ cups buttermilk baking mix
½ cup chopped walnuts or pecans
  Orange Glaze (page 120)

Preheat oven to 350°F. Grease and flour 9-inch square baking pan and set aside.

Beat butter, granulated sugar, egg, and vanilla in medium-size bowl with electric mixer until thoroughly blended. Beat in date filling. Stir in baking mix and walnuts and spread batter evenly in prepared pan.

Bake 40 to 45 minutes or until toothpick inserted in center comes out clean. Cool completely in pan on wire rack.

Spoon or drizzle Orange Glaze over cooled cake. Let stand until glaze is set. Cut into nine 3-inch squares and remove from pan.

9 squares

Easy SPITZER'S TORTE

1 box (18¼ ounces) white or
  chocolate cake mix
3 eggs
⅓ cup vegetable oil
1 cup water
¼ cup light rum or brandy

2 cans Solo or 2 jars Baker Cherry
  Filling, divided
1 container (16 ounces) ready-to-
  spread vanilla frosting, divided
About ⅔ cup sliced almonds

Preheat oven to 350°F. Grease and flour two 9-inch round cake pans and set aside.

Prepare and bake cake mix according to package directions, using whole eggs, oil, water, and rum. Cool in pans on wire racks 15 minutes. Remove from pans and cool completely on racks. Cut each layer in half horizontally to make 4 layers.

Set ½ container cherry filling aside. Place 1 cake layer, bottom side up, on serving plate and spread with ½ container cherry filling. Top with second layer and spread with ½ container cherry filling. Top with third layer and spread with ½ container cherry filling. Top with fourth layer and press down gently.

Set ⅓ cup frosting aside to decorate. Brush any loose crumbs off cake. Spread frosting over top and side of cake and smooth with long, thin spatula. Sprinkle almonds around side of cake and press lightly into frosting.

Spoon reserved ½ container cherry filling over top of cake to within ¾ inch of edge all the way around. Spoon reserved ⅓ cup frosting into pastry bag fitted with large open star tip and pipe in border around top edge of cake. Refrigerate until ready to serve.

8 to 10 servings

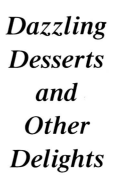

CHAPTER 7

*Dazzling
Desserts
and
Other
Delights*

*Strawberry-Glazed Pears
(page 139), Filled Caribbean
Pound Cake (page 124)*

Easy
FILLED CARIBBEAN POUND CAKE

1 can (8 ounces) crushed pineapple, drained	1 frozen pound cake (16 ounces), partially thawed
1 ripe banana, chopped	1 cup heavy cream
⅓ cup chopped maraschino cherries	2 tablespoons confectioners sugar
¾ cup Solo Fruit Salad Dressing	Quartered maraschino cherries to decorate

Place pineapple, banana, and chopped cherries in medium-size bowl. Stir in fruit salad dressing until fruit is coated. Set aside.

Cut cake into 3 equal-size layers. Place bottom layer on serving plate and spread with half of fruit mixture. Top with second layer and spread with remaining fruit mixture. Top with third layer and press down gently.

Whip cream in medium-size bowl with electric mixer until soft peaks form. Add confectioners sugar and whip until firm. Spread whipped cream over top and around side of cake. Decorate with quartered maraschino cherries. Refrigerate at least 2 hours before serving.

8 servings   *(see photo page 122)*

HAWAIIAN PINEAPPLE COBBLER

2 cans Solo or 2 jars Baker Pineapple Filling	4 tablespoons (¼ cup) sugar, divided
½ cup chopped dates	1½ teaspoons baking powder
½ cup coarsely chopped walnuts	¼ cup butter or margarine
¾ cup light cream, divided	1 tablespoon cinnamon
1 cup all-purpose flour	1 cup apple cider or apple juice
	Heavy cream to serve

Preheat oven to 375°F. Grease 13 x 9-inch baking pan.

Spread pineapple filling in prepared pan. Combine dates and walnuts and scatter over filling. Pour ¼ cup cream over mixture and set aside.

Place flour, 2 tablespoons sugar, and baking powder in medium-size bowl and stir until blended. Cut in butter until mixture resembles coarse crumbs. Stir in remaining ½ cup cream. Drop by heaping tablespoonfuls onto date mixture. Combine remaining 2 tablespoons sugar and cinnamon and sprinkle over dough. Pour apple cider over.

Bake 25 to 30 minutes or until toothpick inserted in center of dough comes out clean.

Serve warm with heavy cream.

8 to 10 servings

QUICK FRUIT CRISP

Quick

2 cans Solo or 2 jars Baker Apple,
  Cherry, or Blueberry Filling
⅔ cup quick-cooking rolled oats
⅓ cup all-purpose flour
¼ cup firmly packed brown sugar

½ teaspoon cinnamon
¼ teaspoon nutmeg
¼ cup butter or margarine, softened
Vanilla ice cream to serve

Preheat oven to 375°F.

Grease 9-inch square baking pan and spoon apple filling into prepared pan. Combine oats, flour, brown sugar, cinnamon, and nutmeg in medium-size bowl. Cut in butter until mixture resembles coarse crumbs. Sprinkle crumb mixture over apple filling.

Bake 25 to 30 minutes or until top is lightly browned. Serve warm, with vanilla ice cream.

6 servings

Microwave Method: Spoon apple filling into greased 9-inch round micro-proof dish. Prepare crumb topping according to directions above and sprinkle over apple filling. Microcook on high (100%) power 6 to 8 minutes or until topping is set. Serve as directed above.

SOLO CHERRY TRIFLE

Easy

1 package (3½ ounces) instant
  vanilla pudding mix
24 plain lady fingers
  (two 3-ounce packages)
1 can Solo or 1 jar Baker
  Cherry Filling
3 tablespoons cream sherry or
  orange juice, divided

⅓ cup Solo Toasted Almond
  Crunch Topping
Sweetened whipped cream or
  frozen non-dairy whipped
  topping, thawed, to decorate

Prepare pudding according to package directions and set aside.

Split lady fingers in half, spread cherry filling over half of them, and sandwich them together. Arrange 12 filled lady fingers in bottom of 2-quart glass serving bowl. Sprinkle with 1½ tablespoons sherry and spread half of pudding over. Arrange remaining 12 filled lady fingers over pudding. Sprinkle with remaining 1½ tablespoons sherry and spread remaining pudding on top.

Sprinkle crunch topping over pudding, decorate with piped whipped cream, and refrigerate several hours or overnight.

8 to 10 servings

GLAZED FRUIT "PIZZA"

1 can Solo Almond Paste
½ cup butter or margarine

1½ cups all-purpose flour
1 to 2 tablespoons cold water

Topping:
1 package (8 ounces) cream
** cheese, softened**
½ cup sugar
1 teaspoon vanilla
2 cups blueberries

2 cups strawberries, cut in half
2 cups sliced peaches
2 kiwifruit, peeled and sliced
1 cup Solo Peach Glaze

Preheat oven to 350°F. Grease 12-inch pizza pan.

Break almond paste into small pieces and place in food processor. Add butter and process until blended. Add flour and process until mixture is crumbly. Add cold water, 1 tablespoon at a time, and process until dough binds together and forms ball. Press dough evenly onto bottom and up side of prepared pan to make rim. Prick crust all over with prongs of fork.

Alternatively, break almond paste into small pieces and place in medium-size bowl. Add butter and beat at medium speed with electric mixer until thoroughly blended. Stir in flour gradually. Add water, 1 tablespoon at a time, until mixture binds together.

Bake 15 to 18 minutes or until golden. Cool in pan on wire rack 15 minutes. Remove crust from pan carefully and place on rack to cool completely.

To make topping, beat cream cheese, sugar, and vanilla in small bowl with electric mixer until blended. Spread over cooled crust with back of metal spoon.

Place blueberries, strawberries, peaches, and kiwifruit in 4 separate bowls. Add ¼ cup peach glaze to each bowl and toss fruit gently to coat. Arrange circles of glazed fruit over cream cheese. Refrigerate until ready to serve.

6 to 8 servings

Variation: Any combination of fresh fruit, canned and drained fruit, or frozen and thawed fruit may be used.

CRÊPES WITH APPLE FILLING

⅔ cup milk
2 eggs
½ cup all-purpose flour
2 tablespoons sugar

¼ teaspoon salt
2 tablespoons unsalted
   butter, melted

Filling:
½ cup raisins
¼ cup Calvados or apple juice
1 can Solo or 1 jar Baker
   Apple Filling

½ teaspoon cinnamon
¼ cup chopped walnuts or pecans
3 tablespoons lemon juice
Confectioners sugar

Place milk and eggs in container of blender or food processor. Add flour, sugar, and salt, and process until blended. Add melted butter and process 30 seconds. Pour batter into 2-cup pitcher, cover, and refrigerate 1 hour.

Melt just enough unsalted butter to lightly grease surface of 6- or 7-inch crêpe pan. Stir batter. (If batter is too thick, thin with small amount of additional milk.) Pour 2 to 3 tablespoons batter into greased pan and swirl batter to cover surface of pan in very thin layer. Cook over medium heat about 1 minute on each side. Slide crêpe from pan onto plate. Repeat with remaining batter, adding more butter to pan if necessary.

To make filling, place raisins in small bowl. Stir in Calvados and let stand 5 minutes. Combine apple filling, cinnamon, nuts, and lemon juice in medium-size bowl. Stir in raisins. Preheat oven to 375°F.

Place 1 crêpe on work surface. Spoon about 2 tablespoons apple mixture slightly off center on crêpe. Roll crêpe and place, seam side down, on heatproof serving dish. Repeat with remaining crêpes and apple mixture.

Bake 10 to 15 minutes or just until heated through. Sprinkle with confectioners sugar just before serving.

8 filled crêpes

Easy WHIPPED PRUNE CLOUD

1 can Solo or 1 jar Baker Prune,
   Apricot, or Pineapple Filling
½ cup sugar
1 tablespoon lemon juice

½ teaspoon vanilla
1 package (8 ounces) cream
   cheese, softened
1 cup heavy cream, whipped

Combine prune filling, sugar, and lemon juice in small saucepan. Cook over medium heat until mixture comes to a boil, stirring constantly. Remove from heat and stir in vanilla. Add cream cheese and stir until blended. Spoon into large bowl, cover, and refrigerate 1 hour or until almost set.

Stir 3 tablespoons whipped cream into prune mixture to lighten. Fold in remaining whipped cream and spoon into serving dishes.

4 servings

Easy   POPPY NOODLE PUDDING

½ pound wide noodles
¼ cup butter or margarine, melted
½ cup raisins
3 eggs
½ cup sugar

1 can Solo or 1 jar Baker
    Poppy Filling
1 teaspoon cinnamon
2 cups dairy sour cream

Cook noodles according to package directions. Drain well and place in large bowl. Add melted butter and raisins and stir gently until noodles are coated. Set aside.

Preheat oven to 350°F. Grease 2- to 2½-quart casserole or baking dish and set aside.

Beat eggs, sugar, poppy filling, and cinnamon with electric mixer until well blended. Add sour cream and beat until blended. Pour over noodles and stir gently. Pour into prepared dish.

Bake 40 to 45 minutes or until center is set. Cool on wire rack. Serve at room temperature or slightly chilled.

8 servings

Easy   POPPY BREAD PUDDING

1 loaf (16 ounces) day-old white
    bread, crusts removed, cubed
2⅓ cups milk
1 can (12 ounces) evaporated milk
3 eggs
1 can Solo or 1 jar Baker
    Poppy Filling

¾ cup sugar
¼ cup butter or margarine, melted
1 teaspoon vanilla
1 teaspoon cinnamon
½ teaspoon nutmeg
Light cream to serve

Preheat oven to 350°F. Grease 13 x 9-inch baking pan.

Place bread cubes in prepared pan and set aside. Place milk, evaporated milk, and eggs in large bowl, and beat with electric mixer until thoroughly blended. Add poppy filling, sugar, butter, vanilla, cinnamon, and nutmeg, and beat until well mixed. Pour over bread.

Bake 45 to 55 minutes or until tip of knife inserted in center comes out clean. Cool in pan on wire rack.

Serve warm or cold with light cream.

12 servings

APPLE CHIFFON
WITH CRUNCH TOPPING

1 envelope unflavored gelatin	1 can Solo or 1 jar Baker
⅓ cup sugar	Apple Filling
¼ cup apple juice or cider	1 to 2 tablespoons apple-flavored
1 cup milk	brandy (optional)
1 teaspoon cinnamon	½ cup heavy cream
⅛ teaspoon ground cloves	½ to ¾ cup Solo Crunch Topping
2 eggs, separated	(any kind)

Combine gelatin and sugar in medium-size saucepan. Add apple juice and milk and stir until blended. Cook over low heat, stirring, until gelatin and sugar are completely dissolved. Stir in cinnamon and cloves.

Beat egg yolks in small bowl. Add 3 tablespoons hot milk mixture slowly to beaten egg yolks and stir until blended. Return mixture to saucepan and cook, stirring constantly, until mixture thickens and coats back of spoon. (Do not allow mixture to boil.) Remove from heat and pour into medium-size bowl. Let cool 2 minutes. Beat at high speed with electric mixer 3 minutes. Fold in apple filling. Stir in brandy, if desired.

Whip cream in medium-size bowl with electric mixer until firm. Fold into apple mixture. Beat egg whites in separate bowl just until soft peaks form. Fold into apple mixture.

Spoon chiffon into 6 to 8 individual dessert dishes or stem glasses. Refrigerate 3 to 4 hours or until well chilled. Just before serving, sprinkle each serving with crunch topping.

6 to 8 servings

Quick

AMBROSIA

1 can (11 ounces) mandarin oranges	1 cup green or red seedless
1 can (8 ounces) crushed	grapes, halved
pineapple, drained	1 cup shredded or flaked coconut
	½ cup Solo Fruit Salad Dressing

Drain oranges, reserving ¼ cup juice. Place oranges, pineapple, grapes, and coconut in medium-size bowl and toss gently. Combine reserved juice and fruit salad dressing and stir into fruit-coconut mixture. Refrigerate 2 to 3 hours or until ready to serve.

4 to 6 servings

CHOCOLATE APRICOT MOUSSE

2 tablespoons cornstarch
⅔ cup granulated sugar
3 tablespoons unsweetened
   cocoa powder
1¼ cups milk
2 egg yolks

1 can Solo or 1 jar Baker
   Apricot Filling
2 to 3 tablespoons apricot-flavored
   brandy or apricot nectar
1 cup heavy cream
1 teaspoon vanilla
2 tablespoons confectioners sugar

Combine cornstarch, granulated sugar, and cocoa powder in medium-size saucepan. Add milk and stir until blended and smooth. Place saucepan over low heat and cook, stirring, until mixture thickens and comes to a boil.

Beat egg yolks in small bowl. Add 3 tablespoons hot chocolate mixture slowly to beaten egg yolks and stir until blended. Return mixture to saucepan and cook, stirring constantly, until mixture thickens and coats back of spoon. (Do not allow mixture to boil.) Remove from heat and pour into medium-size bowl. Add apricot filling and brandy and stir well. Press sheet of waxed paper over surface of custard to prevent skin from forming. Refrigerate 1 hour.

Whip cream in medium-size bowl with electric mixer until soft peaks form. Add vanilla and confectioners sugar and whip until firm. Set 1 cup whipped cream aside. Fold remaining cup whipped cream into custard. Spoon into 6 individual dessert dishes or serving bowl. Chill 2 to 3 hours or until ready to serve. To serve, top with dollops of reserved whipped cream.

6 servings

Quick PINEAPPLE RICE PUDDING

2 cups cooked rice (short grain
   rice preferred)
1 teaspoon vanilla
1 can Solo or 1 jar Baker
   Pineapple Filling
½ cup coarsely chopped
   maraschino cherries

1 container (8 ounces) frozen
   non-dairy whipped topping,
   thawed, or 1 cup heavy cream,
   whipped and sweetened to taste
Maraschino cherries to decorate

Place rice in medium-size bowl and stir in vanilla and pineapple filling until blended. Fold in chopped cherries and whipped topping. Spoon into individual dessert dishes. Cover and refrigerate at least 2 to 3 hours or until ready to serve. Decorate each serving with cherry.

6 to 8 servings

Chocolate Apricot Mousse, Pineapple Rice Pudding (opposite)

RASPBERRY CUSTARD PARFAITS

Vanilla Custard:

½ cup sugar
3 tablespoons cornstarch
2 cups light cream or half and half

4 egg yolks
1½ teaspoons vanilla

Topping:

1 can Solo or 1 jar Baker Raspberry,
Cherry, or Blueberry Filling

To make custard, stir sugar and cornstarch in medium-size saucepan until mixed. Add cream and beat with wire whisk until smooth. Cook over medium heat until mixture thickens and comes to a boil. Remove from heat. Beat egg yolks in small bowl. Add ½ cup hot cream mixture to beaten egg yolks in slow, steady stream, beating constantly. Return mixture to saucepan and stir to blend. Cook over low heat, stirring constantly, until mixture thickens and coats back of spoon. (Do not allow mixture to boil.)

Pour custard into medium-size bowl and stir in vanilla. Press piece of waxed paper onto surface of custard to prevent skin from forming. Set aside to cool completely.

Spoon 2 tablespoons cooled custard into 4 parfait or sherbet glasses. Spoon layer of raspberry filling over custard. Repeat with layers of custard and filling. Refrigerate 2 to 3 hours or until well chilled.

4 servings

COLD STRAWBERRY SOUFFLÉ

1 envelope unflavored gelatin
½ cup water
½ cup sugar
4 eggs, separated
1 tablespoon lemon juice
2 to 3 tablespoons fruit-flavored
brandy (optional)

1 can Solo or 1 jar Baker Strawberry
Filling or any flavor Fruit Filling
1 cup heavy cream
Sweetened whipped cream and
fresh berries to decorate
(optional)

Cut piece of aluminum foil or waxed paper large enough to fit around 1-quart soufflé dish. Fold foil in half lengthwise, grease 1 side of foil lightly with butter, and sprinkle with sugar, if desired. Wrap around outside of dish, greased side in, extending at least 3 inches above rim of dish to make collar. Secure collar with tape.

Sprinkle gelatin over water in small saucepan and let stand 5 minutes. Cook over low heat, stirring, until gelatin is completely dissolved. Add sugar and stir until dissolved.

Beat egg yolks in small bowl. Stir a little hot liquid slowly into beaten egg yolks. Return mixture to saucepan and cook over low heat, stirring constantly, until mixture thickens and coats back of spoon. (Do not allow mixture to come to a boil.) Pour into large bowl and stir in lemon juice, brandy, and strawberry filling. Cover and refrigerate 30 to 40 minutes or until mixture mounds when dropped from spoon.

Whip cream in medium-size bowl with electric mixer until firm. Fold whipped cream into chilled strawberry mixture.

Beat egg whites in separate bowl with electric mixer until stiff peaks form. Fold into strawberry mixture. Pour into prepared soufflé dish. Refrigerate 3 to 4 hours or until firm.

To serve, remove collar carefully. Decorate top of soufflé with piped whipped cream and fresh berries, if desired. Serve with cookies or spooned over slices of pound cake.

6 servings

CHERRY ALMOND MALAKOFF

1 can Solo Almond Paste	**7 to 8 plain lady fingers, split**
1 cup unsalted butter, softened	**¼ cup Kirsch or cherry-flavored**
⅔ cup sugar	**brandy**
1½ cups heavy cream	**Maraschino cherries with stems**
2 cans Solo or 2 jars Baker	**to decorate**
Cherry Filling	

Grease 2-quart charlotte mold or soufflé dish. Line bottom of mold with waxed paper and grease paper. Set aside.

Break almond paste into small pieces and place in medium-size bowl or container of food processor. Add butter and beat with electric mixer or process until mixture is creamy and smooth. Add sugar and beat until mixture is light and fluffy. (If using food processor, transfer mixture to medium-size bowl.)

Whip cream in medium-size bowl with electric mixer until firm. Fold whipped cream into almond mixture. Fold in cherry filling.

Brush flat side of lady fingers with Kirsch and line prepared mold with lady fingers, rounded side out. Trim tops of lady fingers even with top of mold. Spoon cherry mixture into center of mold and smooth top. Cover with plastic wrap and refrigerate several hours or until ready to serve.

To unmold, rinse dish towel in hot running water and wring dry. Wrap hot towel around outside of mold and invert mold onto serving plate. Remove mold and peel off lining paper. Decorate top of Malakoff with maraschino cherries.

8 to 12 servings

Quick

RASPBERRY YOGURT DESSERT SOUP

1 can Solo or 1 jar Baker Raspberry,	2 tablespoons lemon juice
Cherry, Strawberry, or	1 container (16 ounces) plain yogurt
Blueberry Filling	Fresh raspberries and mint leaves
3 cups raspberry-cranberry drink	to decorate

Place raspberry filling in medium-size bowl. Add raspberry-cranberry drink and lemon juice and stir until thoroughly blended. Refrigerate 1 hour.

Add yogurt to raspberry mixture and beat with wire whisk until blended and no white streaks remain. Refrigerate 2 hours or until ready to serve.

To serve, ladle into dessert bowls and decorate with fresh raspberries and mint leaves.

6 servings

Easy

FROZEN STRAWBERRY VODKA SHERBET

1 can Solo or 1 jar Baker Strawberry,	2 egg whites
Raspberry, or Cherry Filling	2 tablespoons superfine or
½ cup orange juice	granulated sugar
½ cup vodka, Champagne, or white	Sliced strawberries and fresh mint
grape juice	leaves to decorate

Place strawberry filling in medium-size bowl. Add orange juice and vodka and stir until thoroughly blended. Set aside.

Beat egg whites in medium-size bowl with electric mixer until soft peaks form. Add sugar and beat until stiff and glossy. Add strawberry mixture to beaten egg whites and beat until thoroughly incorporated. Pour mixture into 9-inch square metal or glass pan, cover, and freeze 2 hours.

Line 12-cup muffin pan with foil or paper cupcake liners. Spoon chilled mixture into bowl and beat with electric mixer 2 minutes. Spoon into lined muffin cups, cover muffin pan loosely, and freeze 4 to 5 hours or overnight.

To serve, remove sherbet from pan and peel off cupcake liners. Place 2 balls of sherbet in rounded Champagne glass or dessert dish and decorate with sliced strawberries and fresh mint leaves.

6 servings

Raspberry Yogurt Dessert Soup (opposite)

CRUNCH-TOPPED RASPBERRY MOUSSE

1 envelope unflavored gelatin
½ cup granulated sugar
4 eggs, separated
⅔ cup orange juice or cold water
1 can Solo or 1 jar Baker Raspberry, Strawberry, or Apricot Filling
2 to 3 tablespoons raspberry-flavored liqueur (optional)

1½ cups heavy cream
3 tablespoons confectioners sugar
1 cup Solo Toasted Almond Crunch Topping
4 squares (4 ounces) semisweet chocolate, finely chopped

Combine gelatin and granulated sugar in top of double boiler. Beat egg yolks and orange juice in small bowl until blended. Add to gelatin mixture and beat until well combined. Set double boiler over pan of barely simmering water. Cook, stirring, until mixture thickens and coats back of spoon. Pour into large bowl. Add raspberry filling and liqueur, if desired, and stir until blended. Refrigerate 25 minutes or until mixture mounds when dropped from spoon.

Whip cream in medium-size bowl with electric mixer until soft peaks form. Add confectioners sugar and whip until firm. Fold whipped cream into raspberry mixture.

Beat egg whites in separate bowl with electric mixer until stiff peaks form. Fold into raspberry mixture.

Combine toasted almond crunch topping and chopped chocolate in small bowl. Spoon one-fourth of chocolate crunch mixture into bottom of 1½- or 2-quart soufflé dish. Cover with one-third of raspberry mixture. Sprinkle with one-fourth of chocolate crunch mixture and top with one-third of raspberry mixture. Repeat layers once, and top with remaining one-fourth of chocolate crunch mixture. Refrigerate 3 to 4 hours or until ready to serve.

6 to 8 servings

Easy
STRAWBERRY ICE CREAMWICHES

1½ cups crisp rice cereal
1 cup shredded or flaked coconut
½ cup chopped nuts
¼ cup firmly packed brown sugar

¼ cup butter or margarine, melted
1½ quarts vanilla ice cream, softened
1 can Solo or 1 jar Baker Strawberry or Raspberry Filling

Grease 8-inch square pan and set aside.

Place cereal, coconut, nuts, brown sugar, and butter in medium-size bowl and stir to mix. Pat half of mixture in prepared pan. Spread ice cream evenly over mixture. Sprinkle remaining cereal mixture over and press lightly into ice cream. Cover and place in freezer until firm.

When ready to serve, spread strawberry filling over top and cut into sixteen 2-inch squares.

16 squares

FRUIT ICE CREAM

1½ cups milk, half and half, or
  light cream
¾ cup sugar
¼ teaspoon salt
3 egg yolks, beaten

2 teaspoons vanilla
2 cups heavy cream
2 cans Solo or 2 jars Baker Fruit
  Filling (any flavor)

Combine milk, sugar, and salt in medium-size heavy saucepan and beat until mixture is smooth. Beat in egg yolks until thoroughly blended. Cook over low heat, beating constantly, until mixture is thickened and coats back of spoon. (Do not allow mixture to come to a boil.) Remove from heat, pour into large bowl, and stir in vanilla. Press sheet of waxed paper over surface of custard to prevent skin from forming. Refrigerate 2 hours.

Whip cream in medium-size bowl with electric mixer until almost firm. Fold into chilled custard. Pour mixture into ice cream freezer and process according to manufacturer's instructions. Add fruit filling to mixture when almost firm. Stir until blended and freeze until completely firm.

About 2 quarts

CRUNCHY POPSICLES

1 cup milk, divided
1 envelope unflavored gelatin
⅔ cup sugar
2 teaspoons vanilla
2 cups heavy cream

1 can Solo Peanut Brittle Crunch
  Topping or Toasted Almond
  Crunch Topping
10 (5-ounce) paper cups
10 popsicle sticks

Coating:
⅔ cup semisweet chocolate morsels
  or peanut butter morsels

2 teaspoons vegetable shortening

Sprinkle gelatin over ¼ cup milk in small saucepan and let stand 5 minutes. Place saucepan over low heat. Add sugar and remaining ¾ cup milk. Cook, stirring, until gelatin and sugar are completely dissolved. Pour into large bowl and set aside until completely cool. Stir in vanilla. Refrigerate until mixture mounds when dropped from spoon, about 45 minutes.

Whip cream in separate bowl with electric mixer until firm. Fold peanut brittle crunch topping into chilled milk mixture. Fold in whipped cream. Spoon mixture into ten 5-ounce paper cups, filling each cup about three-quarters full. Place filled cups on small baking sheet or in baking pan. Insert popsicle stick into center of each cup. Freeze until firm, about 3 hours.

To coat, melt chocolate and shortening in small saucepan over low heat and stir until smooth. Remove from heat and cool slightly. Peel paper cups off popsicles. Spoon about 1 teaspoon melted chocolate over top of each popsicle, letting chocolate run down sides. Serve immediately or return to freezer.

10 popsicles

Easy   CARAMEL CRUNCH APPLES

4 to 5 medium-size apples
  (MacIntosh, Rome, or Delicious)
1 package (14 ounces) vanilla or
  chocolate caramels

2 tablespoons water
1 can Solo Crunch Topping
  (any kind)
5 lollipop or popsicle sticks

Line baking sheet with waxed paper or aluminum foil. Lightly grease paper and set aside.

Wash apples and dry thoroughly with paper towels. Insert lollipop or popsicle stick into stem end of each apple. Set aside.

Place caramels in top of double boiler set over pan of simmering water. Add water and cook, stirring constantly, until caramels are melted and mixture is smooth. Remove top of double boiler from heat.

Dip apples into melted caramel, 1 at a time, covering apples completely. Roll in crunch topping immediately. Place on greased paper and let stand until caramel is set.

4 to 5 apples

Quick   # GLAZED FRUIT CUP

1 jar Solo Peach Glaze
1 container (8 ounces) plain or
   lemon yogurt
1 pint ripe strawberries, hulled
   and sliced

1 pint blueberries
1 pint raspberries
1 large banana, sliced

Combine peach glaze and yogurt in small bowl and set aside.

Place strawberries, blueberries, raspberries, and banana in large bowl and toss gently to mix. Pour glaze mixture over fruit and stir gently until fruit is evenly coated. Cover and refrigerate 2 to 3 hours until chilled.

8 servings

Easy   # STRAWBERRY-GLAZED PEARS

4 cups dry white wine or white
   grape juice
2 cups sugar
2 cinnamon sticks

6 firm, ripe Anjou or Bosc
   pears, peeled
1 can Solo or 1 jar Baker Strawberry
   or Raspberry Filling
6 mint sprigs to decorate (optional)

Line jelly-roll pan with waxed paper. Place wire rack over waxed paper and set aside.

Combine wine, sugar, and cinnamon sticks in large saucepan or Dutch oven. Bring to a boil over medium heat. Arrange whole pears on their sides in hot syrup and add enough hot water to cover pears, about 1 cup.

Reduce heat to low. Cover and simmer just until pears are tender. (When properly poached, pears will pierce easily with tip of knife.) Remove pears with slotted spoon and place upright on wire rack to drain. Let cool.

Place pears in individual serving dishes and spoon strawberry filling over. Decorate with sprigs of mint.

6 servings   *(see photo pages 122-23)*

Quick
PEACH FLOAT

2 cups orange sherbet   1 cup milk
1 jar Solo Peach Glaze   4 scoops vanilla ice cream

Place sherbet, peach glaze, and milk in container of blender or food processor. Process until smooth.

Pour into 4 tall, chilled glasses. Top each float with 1 scoop ice cream. Serve immediately.

4 servings

Quick
STRAWBERRY MILK SHAKE

2 cups milk   2 scoops vanilla ice cream
1 can Solo or 1 jar Baker Strawberry,   2 to 4 ice cubes
  Raspberry, Cherry, or Blueberry
  Filling, or 1 jar Solo Peach Glaze

Place milk, strawberry filling, ice cream, and ice cubes in container of blender or food processor and process until smooth. Pour into tall glasses and serve immediately.

2 servings

Quick
SPARKLING CITRUS COOLER

¾ cup milk   1 cup lemon-flavored soda or
1 cup Solo Fruit Salad Dressing   ginger ale
2 scoops vanilla ice cream   Cracked ice cubes (optional)

Place milk, fruit salad dressing, ice cream, and soda in container of blender. Process until smooth and creamy. Add 2 or 3 cracked ice cubes, if desired, and process until slushy.

2 servings

TORTONI

1 can (14 ounces) sweetened
condensed milk
3 egg yolks
¼ cup dark rum or cream sherry, or
1 teaspoon rum extract
2 teaspoons vanilla or 1 teaspoon
almond extract

1 cup Solo Toasted Almond Crunch
Topping, divided
½ cup toasted slivered almonds
⅓ cup chopped maraschino cherries
2 cups heavy cream, whipped

Line two 12-cup muffin pans with foil cupcake liners and set aside.

Beat milk, egg yolks, rum, and vanilla in large bowl with electric mixer until thoroughly blended. Stir in ⅔ cup toasted almond crunch topping, slivered almonds, and maraschino cherries.

Fold whipped cream into egg yolk mixture until no white streaks remain. Spoon mixture into lined muffin cups, filling cups almost to top.

Freeze several hours or until firm. Sprinkle remaining ⅓ cup crunch topping over Tortoni just before serving.

24 Tortoni

Quick BRANDIED FRUIT SAUCE

1 can Solo or 1 jar Baker Apricot,
Raspberry, Strawberry,
Blueberry, or Pineapple Filling
½ cup orange juice

1 tablespoon lemon juice
2 to 3 tablespoons fruit-flavored
brandy

Place apricot filling, orange juice, and lemon juice in small saucepan. Cook over low heat, stirring, until mixture is hot. Remove from heat and let cool slightly. Stir in brandy.

Serve warm or cold over Fruit Ice Cream (page 137) or over plain cake.

About 1½ cups

Quick PEANUT BRITTLE POPCORN

¼ cup sugar	6 to 7 cups popped popcorn
¼ cup light corn syrup	½ cup Solo Peanut Brittle
2 tablespoons butter or margarine	Crunch Topping
2 tablespoons peanut butter	Salt to taste (optional)

Place sugar, corn syrup, and butter in small saucepan and cook over medium heat, stirring, until sugar is dissolved and mixture comes just to a boil. Remove from heat and stir in peanut butter until blended.

Place popcorn in large serving bowl and sprinkle with peanut brittle crunch topping. Add warm peanut butter mixture and toss to coat. Sprinkle with salt, if desired.

6 to 7 cups

Microwave Method: Place sugar, corn syrup, and butter in 2-cup glass measure. Microcook on high (100%) power 2 to 3 minutes or until sugar is dissolved and mixture is hot, stirring after 1 minute. Proceed as directed above.

Quick
CHOCOLATE NUT CRUNCH CLUSTERS

1 pound milk chocolate, coarsely chopped	2 cups coarsely chopped almonds, pecans, walnuts, or hazelnuts
1 can (5 ounces) evaporated milk	1 can Solo Toasted Almond Crunch Topping

Line 2 baking sheets with aluminum foil and set aside.

Place chocolate and evaporated milk in medium-size heavy saucepan. Cook over low heat, stirring constantly, until chocolate is melted and mixture is smooth. Remove from heat and let cool slightly. Add chopped nuts and almond crunch topping and stir until well mixed.

Drop mixture by teaspoonfuls onto foil-lined baking sheets. Let stand at room temperature until completely cool and chocolate is set. Peel candy off foil.

About 2 pounds candy

Microwave Method: Line 2 baking sheets with aluminum foil and set aside. Place chocolate in 4-cup glass measure or medium-size microproof bowl and microcook on high (100%) power 4 minutes, stirring after 2 minutes. Remove from oven and stir until chocolate is smooth. Stir in evaporated milk until blended. Proceed as directed above.

Easy

GRANOLA CRUNCH

6 cups quick-cooking rolled oats	½ cup wheat germ
1 jar (8 ounces) dry-roasted peanuts, coarsely chopped	½ cup sesame seed
1 can Solo Crunch Topping (any kind)	½ cup butter or margarine
	½ cup honey
	1 teaspoon vanilla

Preheat oven to 325°F. Grease 15 x 10-inch jelly-roll pan and set aside.

Place oats, peanuts, crunch topping, wheat germ, and sesame seed in large bowl. Stir until blended. Place butter, honey, and vanilla in small saucepan. Cook over medium heat, stirring, until mixture comes to a boil and butter is melted. Pour over oat mixture in slow, steady stream, stirring with wooden spoon until mixture is well coated. Spoon into prepared pan.

Bake 25 to 30 minutes or until golden brown, stirring every 10 minutes. Cool in pan on wire rack 30 minutes. Store in airtight containers.

About 8 cups crunch

PEANUT BRITTLE CRUNCH FUDGE

2 cups granulated sugar	1 package (6 ounces) butterscotch-flavored morsels
1 cup firmly packed brown sugar	1 package (6 ounces) semisweet chocolate morsels
⅔ cup evaporated milk	½ cup Solo Peanut Brittle Crunch Topping
⅔ cup butter or margarine	
1 jar (7 ounces) marshmallow crème	
1 teaspoon vanilla	

Grease 9-inch square pan and set aside.

Place sugars, evaporated milk, and butter in large saucepan. Cook over medium heat until butter is melted and mixture comes to a boil, stirring constantly. Boil until mixture registers 234°F on candy thermometer (soft ball stage), stirring constantly.

Remove from heat. Add marshmallow crème and vanilla and stir until blended. Pour half of mixture into bowl. Add butterscotch morsels and stir until morsels are melted. Pour into prepared pan.

Add chocolate morsels to remaining mixture and stir until morsels are melted. Spread chocolate mixture carefully over butterscotch layer. Sprinkle peanut brittle crunch topping over and press lightly in place with back of spoon. Let stand at room temperature until completely cool. Cut into about thirty-six 1½-inch squares.

36 squares

MARZIPAN

1 can (8 ounces) Solo Almond Paste	About 2 to 2½ cups
1 egg white	confectioners sugar

Break almond paste into small pieces and place in medium-size bowl. Add egg white and 1 cup confectioners sugar. Knead in bowl until mixture binds together and is no longer crumbly. Sprinkle clean work surface with confectioners sugar. Place marzipan on sugared surface and knead in 1 to 1½ cups confectioners sugar. Continue kneading until marzipan is smooth and pliable. Shape into thick log or block. Wrap tightly in plastic wrap or waxed paper and store in refrigerator. Use to make candy, cake decorations, small marzipan figures, fruit, or to roll out and cover cakes.

About 1¼ pounds

MARZIPAN TRUFFLES

1 recipe Marzipan (above)	1 pound top-quality milk or
About 3 cups confectioners	semisweet chocolate,
sugar	coarsely chopped
2 tablespoons unsweetened	1 can Solo Crunch Topping
cocoa powder	(any kind), crushed
2 teaspoons brandy extract	
1 teaspoon vegetable shortening	

Divide marzipan in half. Wrap 1 piece in plastic wrap and refrigerate. Sprinkle work surface and hands with confectioners sugar. Knead remaining marzipan on sugared surface until pliable. Shape into 12 x 1-inch log. Dust with confectioners sugar, wrap in plastic wrap, and refrigerate overnight.

Break remaining marzipan into small pieces and place on work surface or in food processor. Add cocoa and brandy extract and knead or process until thoroughly blended. Remove from food processor, if necessary. Sugar work surface and knead 1 cup confectioners sugar into mixture. Divide chocolate marzipan in half. Shape each piece into 8 x ¾-inch log. Dust with confectioners sugar and wrap in plastic wrap. Refrigerate overnight.

Line 2 baking sheets with waxed paper and set aside.

Unwrap plain marzipan and place on sugared surface. Cut log into about ½-inch-thick slices. Roll between sugared palms to make balls, place on prepared baking sheet, and refrigerate.

Unwrap chocolate marzipan, 1 log at a time, and place on sugared surface. Cut log into ½-inch-thick slices. Roll between sugared palms to make balls and place on prepared baking sheet. Repeat with remaining chocolate marzipan and refrigerate.

To coat marzipan balls, place shortening and half of chopped chocolate in top of double boiler set over pan of barely simmering water. Cook, stirring constantly, until chocolate is melted. Add remaining chopped chocolate and stir until chocolate is completely melted and mixture is smooth. Remove top of double boiler from pan and set aside to cool slightly.

1: *Dip marzipan balls into melted chocolate and shake off excess chocolate.*

2: *Place the dipped and crunch-coated truffles on a waxed paper-lined baking sheet. Let stand until set.*

Remove 1 tray of marzipan balls from refrigerator. Dip balls, 1 at a time, into melted chocolate and shake off excess chocolate. Return chocolate-dipped balls to lined baking sheet and let stand at room temperature until chocolate is completely set. Dip remaining balls in chocolate, shake off excess chocolate, and roll in crunch topping. Return to lined baking sheet and let stand until chocolate is set. Place truffles in paper bonbon cases and store in refrigerator.

About 56 truffles

Note: If chocolate should harden, place in double boiler and reheat until melted.

MOLDING MARZIPAN
(See photos pages 148-49)

1 recipe Marzipan (page 144)
Food coloring

Confectioners sugar
Light corn syrup

Equipment Needed:
Small paintbrushes
Plastic wrap

Sharp knife and small cutters

To Tint Marzipan: Knead food coloring into small amounts of marzipan on sugared surface before shaping, or paint shapes with small paintbrush after they have been made. To paint marzipan shapes, add a few drops of food coloring to a small amount of water, paint shapes, and set aside to dry on tray.

To Glaze Marzipan: Place ½ cup light corn syrup and 1 cup water in small saucepan. Cook over medium heat, stirring occasionally, until mixture comes to a full rolling boil. Boil rapidly 1 minute. Remove from heat and set aside until completely cool. (Do not stir.) Brush glaze on dry marzipan shapes and let stand on tray until glaze is set.

Marzipan Leaves: Knead green food coloring into marzipan and shape into log about ¾ inch thick. Cut log into ½-inch-thick slices. Press slices into oval shapes and cut into leaf shapes with sharp knife or miniature leaf cutter. Use knife to score veins on leaves. Let dry on tray and brush with glaze, if desired.

Marzipan Roses: Spoon few drops red food coloring on block of marzipan and knead on sugared surface until uniform in color. Shape marzipan into 1-inch-thick log and cut into ½-inch-thick slices. Cut 2 or 3 slices into small pea-size pieces. Shape small pieces into tapered cones with flat bottoms to be used for centers of roses. To make petals, place several marzipan slices between two sheets of plastic wrap and flatten with thumb, making edges of each petal very thin. Peel off top sheet of plastic wrap, pick up 1 petal with tip of sharp knife, and wrap around marzipan cone. Press bottom of petal firmly onto cone and curl back top edge of petal carefully. Repeat, adding as many petals as desired. Be sure each row of petals is placed slightly below row above. Set roses aside on tray to dry. Brush with glaze, if desired.

Marzipan Fruit:

Apples: Break or cut green-tinted marzipan into 1-inch pieces. Shape each piece into slightly flattened round ball. Insert whole clove for stem. Paint diluted red food coloring around apple. Let dry on tray. Brush with glaze, if desired.

Oranges: Mix red and yellow food coloring to make orange. Tint marzipan and cut or break into walnut-size pieces. Shape into oranges. Roll oranges gently over surface of grater to make rough surface. Insert whole clove for stem. Let dry on tray. Brush with glaze, if desired.

Lemons: Cut or break deep-yellow-tinted marzipan into walnut-size pieces. Shape into tapered ovals. Roll lemons gently over surface of grater to make rough surface. Insert whole clove at each end. Let dry on tray. Brush with glaze, if desired.

Bananas: Break or cut yellow-tinted marzipan into 1½-inch pieces. Shape into bananas. Brush thin lines of diluted brown food coloring on bananas. Let dry on tray. Brush with glaze, if desired.

Strawberries: Cut or break deep-red-tinted marzipan into 1-inch pieces. Shape into strawberries. Roll strawberries gently over surface of grater to make rough surface. Glaze and roll lightly in sugar for crystallized effect. Roll out green-tinted marzipan to about ⅛-inch thickness and cut out small star shapes or small petals. Attach to top of strawberries with drop of sugar glaze. Let dry on tray. Brush with glaze, if desired.

Cherries: Mix red and blue food coloring to make deep red cherry color. Tint marzipan and cut or break into ¾-inch pieces. Roll into balls. Use blunt edge of knife to make crease in cherry. Insert stem from maraschino cherry or use green-tinted marzipan leaf. Let dry on tray. Brush with glaze, if desired.

Apricots: Mix red and yellow food coloring to make light orange. Tint marzipan and cut or break marzipan into walnut-size pieces. Shape into slightly oval balls. Use blunt edge of knife to make crease in apricot. Lightly brush diluted brown food coloring around sides of apricots, if desired. Attach green-tinted marzipan leaf to top of apricots with drop of glaze. Let dry on tray. Brush with glaze, if desired.

Hints and Tips for Molding Marzipan:

● If marzipan has been refrigerated, allow it to come to room temperature before molding.

● Sprinkle work surface, rolling pin, and hands generously with confectioners sugar before working with marzipan. Repeat as necessary in order to keep marzipan from sticking to work surface or hands.

● When possible, use paste coloring rather than liquid coloring to tint marzipan.

● Be careful not to overknead marzipan. Overkneading may cause oil in almond paste to separate out and make marzipan greasy.

● Work with small amounts of marzipan. Cover remaining marzipan with plastic wrap or waxed paper to prevent it from drying out and forming a "crust."

● Spread thin film of vegetable oil over metal knife or cutter to prevent marzipan from tearing when cutting out shapes.

● If using small plastic molds to make marzipan candy, dust molds lightly with cornstarch and tap out excess before pressing marzipan into molds.

● Don't try to mold or paint marzipan on a hot, humid day. Shapes will not dry properly.

● Allow finished marzipan pieces to dry at room temperature before storing.

● Wrap dried marzipan shapes in plastic storage bags and freeze in airtight container up to 6 months. Thaw at room temperature 5 to 6 hours before removing from container and plastic bag. This will prevent moisture from forming on outside of marzipan.

● Don't be afraid to experiment with marzipan shapes. You can always remold them.

● To roll marzipan into large circle or rectangle, roll between 2 large sheets of plastic wrap. Remove top layer of plastic wrap and invert marzipan over cake. Peel off remaining piece of plastic wrap and carefully smooth out wrinkles or folds with fingertips.

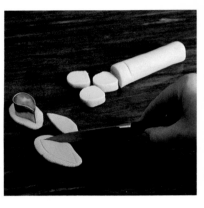

1: *Tools and equipment to make marzipan figures and cutouts: food coloring, paints, brushes, grater, small cutters, rolling pin, knife, marzipan molds, and tinted marzipan.*

2: *Cut small pieces of marzipan to make leaves, using sharp knife or small cutter.*

3: *Score lines on leaves with tip of sharp knife to make veins.*

4: *Shape small pieces into cones to make centers of roses.*

5: *To make rose petals, use thumb to press small pieces between sheets of plastic wrap.*

6: *Use tip of sharp knife to lift petals from work surface.*

7: *Wrap petals around marzipan cone and press bottom of petals firmly to make rose.*

8: *Marzipan fruit can be shaped in molds or by hand.*

Index By Recipe

Index By Product

A $12.95 Value Just $7.95. Order Additional Copies Today.

Please send _____ copies of **A CENTENNIAL CELEBRATION: Recipes from Solo.**
Enclosed is $ _____ ($7.95 per book including postage and handling).

Name _____

Address _____

City _____ State_____ Zip _____

Send name and address, along with check or money order payable
to Sokol & Company (no cash).

Mail to: Solo-Baker, Dept. B
5315 Dansher Road
Countryside, IL, USA 60525-3192
Allow approximately six weeks for delivery.